M

Planet Explorer ★ Dolls ★ Plastic Lipstick

DESIGN

Thomas Hauffe

BARRON'S

For Christine and Greta

American text version by: Editorial Office Sulzer-Reichel, Rösrath, Germany
Translated by: Sally Schreiber, Friedrichshafen, Germany
Edited by: Bessie Blum, Cambridge, Mass.

First edition for the United States and Canada
published by Barron's Educational Series, Inc., 1996.

First published in the Federal Republic of Germany in 1995 by
DuMont Buchverlag GmbH und Co. Kommanditgesellschaft,
Köln, Federal Republic of Germany.

All inquiries should be addressed to:
Barron's Educational Series, Inc.
250 Wireless Boulevard
Hauppauge, New York 11788

Library of Congress Catalog Card No. 96-83721

ISBN 0-8120-9772-6

Printed in Italy by Editoriale Libraria

Contents

Preface   7

Introduction   8

What Is Design?   10

Early History   20
- Industry and technology   20
- Shaker life-style and handcrafts   23
- The Biedermeier age   25

The Industrial Revolution   28
- From workshop to factory   28
- Industrial expansion and historicism   32
- World exhibitions and international competition   34
- *The Thonet Brothers*   36

Reform Movements   38
- William Morris and the arts and crafts movement   41
- Art nouveau, an international movement   43

The Road to Modernism   54
- Mackintosh and the Glasgow School of Art   54
- Vienna at the turn of the century   55
- "Form follows function"   57
- The German Werkbund   60

AEG *Peter Behrens*   62

Revolution and the Avant-Garde   64
- Art into life   64
- Vladimir Tatlin: "The artist as a life-style organizer"   66
- The Netherlands: De Stijl (1917–31)   70
- The Bauhaus (1919–1933)   74
- Social housing in Germany   80
- The "international style"   83

Luxury and Power   86
- Art Deco   88
- Modern industrial design   95
- The streamlined form   97
- Design in the Third Reich   99

The Economic Miracle	104
• Organic design in home furnishings	106
• The American way of life	108
🖼 Raymond Loewy	110
• The Italian economic miracle	112
• Germany:	
From recovery to *Wirtschaftswunder*	116
• The Academy for Design	120
• Scandinavian home design	125
Good Form and Bel Design	128
• Consumption and technology	128
• "Good form" and neo-functionalism	130
🖼 The Braun Corporation	132
• Italy: Bel design	134
• Plastics and polyesters	137
Experimentation and Antidesign	140
• The crisis of functionalism	141
• Pop culture and utopias	144
• Italian countermovements	146
Postmodernism	148
• From modern to postmodern	148
• "Studio Alchimia"	151
• "Memphis"	153
• The "wild eighties"	156
• The New Design	157
• Coming into the nineties	
Design and technology	166
• Design and marketing	170
• Design and culture	171
• Design and the environment	173
• What's ahead?	175
Glossary	176
A chronological history of design	177
Museums and design collections	180
Bibliography	181
Subject index	185
Index of names	188
Picture credits	192

Preface

Design is everywhere. In recent years, design has become a subject of general interest—hardly confined to "serious" journals, it is commonly covered by the general press and even on television, which regularly report on outstanding exhibits, new designs, and the "designer scene." Books on special themes, glitzy articles in life-style magazines, exhibition catalogs, and books that are themselves objects of design flood the market. This popular aspect of design is in addition to exhibitions of individual epochs, such as Art Deco, the "swinging fifties," and even the "wild eighties."

The history of design, like the history of art, has developed into a scholarly field of its own. It is most advanced as such a field in Great Britain, where a "Design History Society" has existed since 1977; the majority of design historians to date are British. Elsewhere, the line between design history and art history is less clear, and design scholars, critics, and students generally come from the academic field of art history. Otherwise, their work emerges in journals, the press, or from the design scene itself. But despite the plethora of publications, it is difficult to find a general introduction to the subject, or even a simple overview of the theme. Certainly, in comparison with the vast field of art history, histories of design are scarce, and one would be better off knowing in advance the narrow field in which one is interested, and then delving into the art history shelves for more information. There is also a gaping chasm between the highly specialized scholarly text, on the one hand, and expensive coffee-table books that are usually lovely to look at, but have very little to say.

This Crash Course on Design should help to fill this gap by offering a readable and organized presentation of the history of design and an introduction into an ever more complicated theme. Richly illustrated, the book makes comparisons and explains underlying international political and cultural connections. No attempt is made here to offer an encyclopedic enumeration of the names of designers and firms; rather, the crash course is "designed" to present a survey of the main lines of development and influential factors. In addition, short "excursions" examining important designers, firms, and decisive turning points in the history of design offer examples of connections that are necessary for the understanding of an epoch, or that have a particular significance in themselves.

To serve as well as a quick reference, the Crash Course includes a glossary, a bibliography of literature and magazines, as well as a guide to design museums and exhibitions throughout the world.

Thomas Hauffe

Introduction

Philippe Starck (1949–, Paris), star of the designer scene in France, presents both himself and his products as a kind of show heretofore expected only from pop music and movie stars.

Design: Between art ...

Design is everywhere. The word is hanging in the air, so to speak—one could almost say we breathe it in with every breath.

Like art and literature, theater and music, design has become a regular theme in the magazine sections of the major newspapers, and in the culture sections of popular magazines and journals. Where the names of the designers of manufactured commodities—aside from the famous fashion designers—were formerly without resonance, today the stars of the design scene are almost as famous as the stars in show business or music. Names like Ettore Sottsass, Philippe Starck, Charles and Ray Eames, and Matteo Thun are as well known as their designs, and famous designers have the aura of art personalities. Firms go so far as to print a designer's name on their products as an artist's signature. To increase the value, and thereby the commercial appeal of their products, "limited" and "signed" editions of chairs, hi-fi's, and glasses have been created. Architects, a special kind of designers, have always had a public name, especially those who have made a reputation for themselves as breakers of new ground: Louis Sullivan, Frank Lloyd Wright, Frank O. Gehry.

Today, design is a recognized field of cultural history. Knowledge of the classics of modern design, meanwhile, has almost become common cultural property, like art, and design objects are similarly presented. After the recent boom in design, the provocative furniture pieces of the New Design of the "wild eighties" already stand in museums alongside Thonet chairs, chrome furniture, and Bauhaus lamps. Design is a cultural event, and great design exhibitions, like great art exhibitions, draw streams of visitors.

... and industry

In industry, design—the determination of a product's form— is no longer the exclusive concern of engineers, but is a significant marketing factor whose importance is an essential component of the business policy of an

Introduction

increasing number of firms. In an age in which many products are technically mature, distinctions in quality no longer really exist in certain market sectors, and the determination of prices for products with approximately the same wage and material costs can hardly vary. Design, thus, becomes the ultimate difference in competitiveness. To design belongs not only the shaping of individual products, but also the image of an entire firm, in everything from the design of its letterhead to its company buildings, from its bags to its advertisements—its so-called corporate identity. An entire "corporate philosophy" needs to be communicated both inside and outside the firm.

Corporate consultants, design centers, and public institutions, as well as economic ministries and chambers of commerce, support this new consciousness of the effect of design through publications, exhibitions, and contests.

The overall presence of design, however, has also led to an inflation of the term. Like a seal of approval, it is applied indiscriminately to all sorts of things to increase their marketability. Suddenly, there are designer jeans, designer glasses, designer furniture, and, to top it all off, designer drugs, none of which has anything to do with the original meaning of the word.

Next to the verbal nonsense, often driven to extremes, in the 1980s weighty and serious discussions arose over the meaning of the term "design" because technical development and new aesthetic ideals were dissolving the borders between art, craft, industry, and design.

Today the question, "What is design?" is almost as difficult to answer as the question, "What is art?" And, because design is influenced in both theory and practice by the most varied factors, it is no longer possible to come up with a single definition. In spite of this, or perhaps because of it, the attempt to mark out the territory of design is important.

Back to art—leaning on Joseph Beuys and Andy Warhol. Siegfried Michael Syniuga, representative of the New German Design, made chairs into cult objects in the 1980s.

9

• Corporate design

• Interface design

• Industrial design

• Interior design

• Public design

• Fashion design

• Furniture design

• Automobile design

• Commercial design

• Conceptual design

• Computer design

• Information design

• Packaging design

• Communications design

• Avant-garde design

• Hardware design

• Tabletop design

• Counter design

• Radical design

• Media design

• Food design

• Anti-design

• Re-design

• Film design

• Sound design

• Object design

• Software design

What is design?

As often as the word design is used today, its meaning is unclear to most people. The media, the advertising industry, and the field of marketing all use the term for completely different purposes, and often refer to totally different aspects of a constantly growing range of meanings. What is behind this confusion?

Design and planning

Etymologically, the word "design" comes from the Italian *disegno*, which since the Renaissance has meant the drafting or drawing of a work, and in general, beyond this, the idea at the root of a work. From here, design was used in England in the 16th century in the sense of a "plan from which something is to be made ... a drawn sketch for an artwork," but also, according to Bernhard Bürdek, already in the sense of "an object of the applied arts."

The industrial revolution

Today we normally use the term design in general for the drafting and planning of industrial products. Thus, we can at least limit the term to the period since the industrial revolution, which began in England, and from there spread to the other countries of the world. With the coming of industrialization, the history of design also begins—around the middle of the 19th century.

Definition of terms

How does one usually define a term? Normally, one presents its essential contents and important characteristics, and distinguishes it from related terms. In the case of design, the attempt is always made to distinguish the term on the one hand from art and on the other from handwork or craft.

In the course of the history of design, there have, of course, been extremely varied notions of

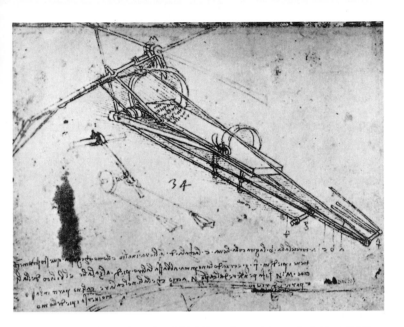

what design is, what tasks it should fulfill, and what should be its major emphases. Considerable contradictions arose, and hefty arguments have broken out repeatedly over the meaning of design. In Germany, prior to 1945, the fashioning of industrial products was not even called design but *Produktgestaltung* ("product shaping") or *industrielle Formgebung* ("industrial form-giving").

Leonardo da Vinci (1452–1519), *Study for a Flying Machine*. In the work of the universal genius, art and technical design are united. For many people, Leonardo ranks as the "first designer."

Assumptions

Both the definitions and the contents have changed. Earlier, the single chief determinant in the definition of design was the industrial production of a product, because with the increased division of labor in the course of industrialization, the first draft of a project and and its actual production no longer lay in the hands of the same person. Thus, industrialization created the basic requirement for the profession of the designer, who later became known as the industrial designer.

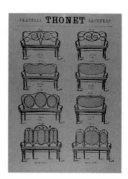

Multilingual *Modellblatt* from an international catalog of the Thonet brothers, 1883.

Closely related to the methods of industrial production was series, as well as mass, production: many everyday objects, such as the variety of pieces of furniture, were not produced as single pieces but in larger quantities. New distribution methods (catalogs, sales representatives, etc.) and increasing use of advertising provided for a high turnover. After the dissolution of many trade and customs barriers in the middle of the 19th century, sales became increasingly international.

Reform movements

Since the early years of industrialization, movements arose, especially in England and Germany, seeking to counter the negative effects of the industrial revolution through reforms in the areas of skilled crafts, social engagement, and development of taste among the general population. One direction of such reform movements was to return decisively to the past, to replace cheap, poor-quality industrial products with qualitatively better products of a reformed skilled craft production. A second direction sought to improve the form and fashion of industrial products by accommodating their form to the requirements of industrial production in order to arrive at modern, inexpensive, durable, and beautiful products.

Thonet Chair No. 14, 1859. Thonet chairs were produced partly by machine, partly by hand from standardized elements that could be used in the assembly of various models. The chairs were easily disassembled for transport to various international sales outlets—one of the reasons for their tremendous success.

"Form follows function"

The moral and social aspects of serial production also led to an aesthetic definition of design, arrived at especially through the theory of functionalism. The supporters of modernism and of functionalism assumed, first, that the form of an object had only to suit its function, and must not include any superfluous ornamentation, and second, that the industrial conditions of production demanded a standardized, simple, geometric language of form in order to be able to produce good-quality and durable products inexpensively, as was necessary for social reform. Until the recent past, the theory of functionalism almost exclusively dictated the aesthetic definition of official industrial design. For a long time, design was synonymous with the simplification of form—and simplification of form with improved usability, higher quality, and a fair price.

The profession of designer

The term "designer" is, of course, not copyrighted; in principle, anyone who plans and makes something can call him or herself a designer. In fact, many of the great designers had no specialized education, but were trained as architects or emerged from the advertising industry. Today, one normally studies industrial design or graphic design at a university or professional college.

The study of industrial design includes the whole spectrum of subjects important for the work of designing: aesthetics, semiotics, color theory, and the like. The analysis and presentation of objects are addressed through a study of geometry, perspective, and proportion. Technical physics, materials science, construction, quality standards, and serialization cover the technical sides of the designing process. A separate field

> "It is only through standardization, which is to be understood as the result of a healthy concentration, that a generally accepted and sure taste can again be established."
> *Hermann Muthesius,* 1914

> "Ornamentation as a rule makes the product more expensive. ... Lack of ornamentation leads to a decrease in production time and a raise in wages. ... Ornament is wasted work effort and therefore wasted wealth."
> *Adolf Loos,* Decoration and Crime, *1908*

"It's getting better for us every day." Photo montage with chairs from 1921–25 by Marcel Breuer (from the magazine *Bauhaus*, vol. 1, 1926). A caption beneath the bottom picture reads: "Finally, one sits on a column of air."

in the study of industrial design is ergonomics, which focuses on the relationship between human beings and their environment. Further, questions of fair and healthful working conditions and safety are also a part of the design education.

There is one area of the education curriculum that concentrates entirely on product planning, that is, on the organizational, economic, legal, and market-oriented questions that arise in connection with the development and marketing of a product. In practice, this area, known as design management, is becoming increasingly important as questions of patents and advertising become a larger part of the industrial effort to establish a competitive advantage.

An introduction to the history and theory of design extends the education of the designer.

The work of the designer has several major focal points: the artistic/aesthetic, the technical/functional, the marketing orientation, the theoretical/scientific, and the organizational/administrative. In practice, these areas all tend to overlap because technical factors are related to economic factors, while aesthetic issues have an impact on marketing.

The concrete applications of design are as varied as the profession itself. Most often, one distinguishes between commercial design and industrial design, although the designation "industrial" hardly seems logical today, since the borders among the different forms of production and organization in most sectors are muddy.

The focus of industrial design extends from articles of daily use, such as furniture, household appliances, household products, and clothing, to the products of the machine, automotive, and airplane industries. Thus, considered closely, not only is the highly visible, "beautiful" world of consumer goods the field of the designer, but so

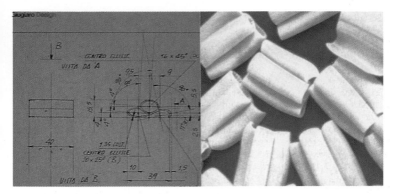

are tanks and rockets, surgical instruments, vibrators, and condoms. In recent years, designers have increasingly discovered areas such as medical technology and the field of rehabilitation. In this way, after being ignored for many years (bespeaking an underlying attitude of unwillingness to confront or to accept different needs among human beings), wheelchairs, invalid beds, and walking aids for the disabled have benefited from improvements in form and function, making such equipment more practical, easier to use, more individual, and no longer necessarily burdened with the stamp of clinical appliances—a clear boon from the psychological point of view.

Graphic design

Graphic, or commercial, design includes all areas of communication, which is why the expression is often used interchangeably with communications design. Once upon a time, it was the responsibility of graphic designers to create posters and placards, advertisements, or the public image of a firm—that is, chiefly work on paper. Today, as communication also takes place by means of the computer screen, the telephone answering machine, and other audio-visual media, the designer is also concerned with

There is nothing without design. Italian designer Giorgio Giugiaro who developed the pasta noodle *Marille* for Voiello, an Italian food manufacturer.

"Design is more than what the economy and production claim for themselves."
François Burkhardt, 1983

Harlan Ross Feltus, advertisement for *Portofino Children's Wear*, 1991. In the fashion sector, fashion design, photography, and graphic design all go hand-in-hand.

the creation of computer programs and protocols of internal corporate communication and information exchange.

The functions of design

Design—the drafting and planning of a product or a service—is a process in which the form of a product comes into existence alongside the determination of its function. "Function" here is not limited to the technical or ergonomic operation, but to an entire web of functions whose effect is aesthetic, semantic, or symbolic communication. As early as 1937, the Czech philosopher Jan Mukarovsky developed a model of five functions for architecture: "the immediate, the historical, the personal, the social, and the aesthetic." Similar theoretical models have emerged continually since then because the connection between form and function has been one of the central, controversial issues in the discussion of the history of design. In design, however, one can speak of three basic functions of an object:

A design by the firm frog-design, 1994. In the age of the digital image, graphic design not only demands clarity, but depth and simultaneity as well, while it both affects and is affected by the environment.

1. its practical, technical function,
2. its aesthetic function, and
3. its symbolic function.

Design as science

Design is a science that draws upon a wide variety of methods from entirely different areas of technology, economics, the social sciences, and the liberal arts. In the course of design history, these areas have been variously evaluated in both the theory and in design. From the functionalism at the beginning of the 20th century until well into the 1970s, the function and the technical requirements of industrial mass production were considered the measuring stick for the form of an industrial product. On the other hand, "styling," which is particularly common in American industrial design, places the marketing aspect in the foreground: here, the attractive shell of a product plays an important role.

By contrast, German design of the 1950s and 1960s was highly technically oriented, putting the emphasis, for example, on the ergonomics of the workplace and the practical convenience of the product. Since the end of the 1960s, especially since we have begun to speak of the "post-modern," the liberal arts have been increasingly incorporated into explanations of the functions of design. With recognition that design not only fulfills technical and material functions but is also a medium of communication, methods from psychology, semantics, and other areas of communication science have been employed in order to investigate and describe the symbolic character of designed objects. A chair is more than a chair: it can, of course, function as a mere tool for sitting, but it can also speak a distinct and universally understood language. As the chair of the boss, it documents social status; as an art object, it reflects the personality of its owner.

Corporate design exemplified by the German airline Lufthansa. From the logo to the shape of the airplane, with its interior appointments, to the uniforms of the crew and their manners toward the public, everything is a part of the firm's corporate image.

Crossing the boundaries

The 1980s witnessed a growing confrontation, first in Italy, then throughout Europe in general and with particular vehemence in Germany, between traditional functionalism and a new designing principle that rejected the old models of design—simplicity, reduction to pure function, and also the definition of industrial mass production. Suddenly, hand-finished prototypes and objects exhibited in galleries and museums were spoken of as objects of a design that was no longer chiefly technical, but was meant to awaken emotions; no longer merely practical, but beautiful—a design that in fact rejected generally accepted standards and distinct patterns of taste. Thus, this new kind of design came surely and provocatively to transgress the old established borders between art, handiwork, and design. At the same time, this different approach to design was facilitated and enhanced by the possibilities of computer-guided machines, which made it possible to derive profit from shorter production runs.

"Kunstflug," *Projection of Styles*, 1988. Design here falls between theory, conceptual art, and social criticism.

Design today

The range of application of design has also changed. Where once only the form of tangible objects was an issue, today everything from computer programs to processes and organizational forms, services, corporate design, and the image of public personalities is designed. The newest field in design is so-called service design, which finds new tasks especially in the constantly growing leisure sector. And, next to designing itself, so-called design management is gaining ever greater importance.

New fields are opening in classic areas of design as well. New factors in industrial design are worth noting: for example, the environmental tolerability of materials and the graphic clarity and user-friendliness of complex service instructions in electronics, where the technical function is no longer concrete, but more and more intangible.

The history of design

When one speaks of the history of design, one is usually referring not only to technical, economic, aesthetic, and social development, but also to psychological, cultural, and ecological aspects. Design history is not merely a chronology of objects and their forms, but a record of the forms of life, because the relation of human beings to the objects they produce and use reflects, especially in the 20th century, a large segment of cultural history.

A model for design and society, adapted from Küthe/Thun, 1995.

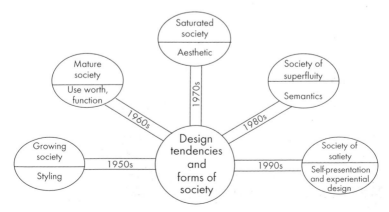

19

1750 – 1850

1752	Benjamin Franklin discovers electricity
1765	James Watt develops the steam engine
1774	The first Shaker community is established in America
1776	Declaration of Independence
1781	Immanuel Kant, *Critique of Pure Reason*
1789	French Revolution, the storming of the Bastille
1804	Napoleon crowns himself emperor in Paris
1805	Death of Friedrich Schiller
1814–15	Congress of Vienna reorganizes Europe
1824	Ludwig van Beethoven completes his *Symphony No. 9*
1830	The first railway is built between Liverpool and Manchester
1844	Samuel Morse sends the first telegram
1847	Karl Marx and Friedrich Engels, *The Communist Manifesto*
1848	California gold rush; March Revolution in Germany
1851	The Great Exhibition in London

Early history

Even if design as we think of it today dates back to the early stages of the industrial revolution, we need to glance back even further to the pre-industrial period if we are to understand certain phenomena in modern design. For even back in the earlier era we can see the development of certain trendsetting forms, methods, and aesthetic models.

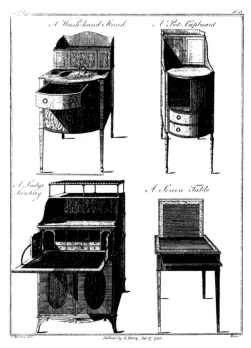

Designs for a washtable and a secretary from Thomas Sheraton's *The Cabinet Maker and Upholsterer's Drawing-Book,* 1791.

Industry and technology

In the process of transition from handwork to industrial production, *conceptual* work—the planning of an object—began to separate itself from work by either hand or machine (i.e., production). Portfolios and pattern books were already being printed and widely distributed in order to solicit and to secure orders; the products themselves, which had formerly been ordered and finished individually according to customer specification, had begun to be standardized. Now furniture, for example, was produced in advance and offered for sale as finished pieces in larger magazines and sales catalogs. Thus, design had early acquired a significance not only for production but for sales.

With the increasing importance of design, the training of the draftsman became more specialized. In addition to classical academies of art, after the middle of the 19th century commercial art schools and museums emerged where collections of these patterns or models were gathered for the purposes of education in both technique and taste. Probably the first nation, and culture, to establish this avenue of training was England, where industrialization had begun at the end of the 18th century, some fifty years before it spread throughout the rest of Europe. The Wedgwood pottery factory, for example, was founded in 1769 by Josiah Wedgwood (1730–95), in the northern city of Stoke on Trent. The distinction of Wedgwood's factory was that it was no longer intended to serve only the demand of the aristocracy, but sought a wider market among the middle class, with more everyday pottery. Wedgwood was, in essence, a pioneer of the mass market, seeing a need and filling it, with "a kind of earthenware table service with a completely new appearance ... which can take sudden changes in temperature, is easy and quick to produce, and is therefore inexpensive." What is remarkable about Wedgwood's efforts is that he tried (and as history would have it, succeeded) to produce earthenware that was both affordable and aesthetically pleasing, using designs by artists such as John Flaxman.

1750 – 1850

Karl Friedrich Schinkel (1781–1841), *Design Drawings for Vessels*, 1821, from his *Portfolio of Patterns for Manufacturers and Handworkers*, published between 1821 and 1837 in Berlin. Pattern and forms modeled after Schinkel were used by most of the workshops and early factories of that time.

1750 – 1850

Office writing cabinet,
Munich, 1815.
A typical example of the
simple furniture of the Biedermeier period, 1814–48.
The Biedermeier style dominated not only its own era,
but continues to influence
style today.

The first-known pattern books of the early
industrial era in Britain come from the two theoreticians of English furniture making, Thomas
Sheraton (1751–1806) and Thomas Chippendale (1718–79) who were to have great
influence throughout Europe. The designs of the
latter were so widely followed that a "Chippendale" today may well be an 18th-century imitation of the originals disseminated via the
pattern books. An original Chippendale, built in
his own workshop, must be authenticated by
means of a paper trail. Though what we think of
today as classic Chippendale style is a rather
ornate kind of carving, with rococo, Chinese,
and Gothic motifs, Thomas Chippendale himself
made furniture in a range of styles, from the
geometrical to the elaborately carved.

Politics and economy
The end of the 18th century and the beginning of
the 19th century in Europe laid the groundwork for
the growth of industry and trade, and hence for
industrial design. The French Revolution (1789),
following the Age of Enlightenment and the American Revolution (1776) with the founding of the
United States on the premise that "All men are

Goethe's workroom in
Weimar. The poet preferred
the simple English furniture of
the time. This style became a
model for German design.

created equal," was the starting point for an increasing ethical and economic self-consciousness within the population. Among the most far-reaching effects of the revolution and the following political new order for Europe after the Congress of Vienna (1814) were the dissolution of many trade and customs barriers, administrative reforms, and the lifting of old guild regulations, all of which strengthened trade and commerce and were a necessary precursor of industrial development.

1750 – 1850

Desk and cabinet of a Shaker community in Harvard, Massachusetts. The furniture was made completely by hand. Its simple and practical form was rooted in the Shakers' religious practice.

Ethics and aesthetics

Among the people, there also developed aesthetic models that still influence design in our own time. The most important requirements of modern design—after functionality, simplicity, and objectivity—arose less from the requirements of production than from the ethic of bourgeois Protestantism, and were less often questions of technique than of religious belief. A prime example of this religion-based aesthetic is seen in the

Guiding Principles of the Shakers
• Regularity is beautiful.
• The highest beauty lies in harmony.
• Beauty arises from practicality.
• Order is the origin of beauty.
• That which is most practical
  is also most beautiful.

simplicity of design of the furniture of the Shakers.

Shaker life-style and handcrafts

A hundred years before the much-quoted formula of Louis Sullivan, "form follows function," pointed the way to the theory of functionalism, the Shaker religious community had laid down among the principles of its faith that "beauty arises from practicality." Originating in England, where they were known as the "Shaking Quakers" (after the

Typical Shaker furniture, ca. 1840: a built-in cabinet with drawers made of walnut and fir wood, a maple rocking chair with a footrest and a cherry candle table. Shaker furniture was plain, functional, and easy to carry, since everything was movable communal property within the community.

1750 – 1850

The round and oval wooden boxes of the Shakers were used to hold a variety of household goods and became a symbol of craftsmanship and detailed perfection. The dove-tailed sides prevented the wood from warping under wet conditions, and the nails are copper instead of iron to prevent rusting.

trembling produced by religious emotion), the Shakers had fled persecution in England, under the leadership of their founder Ann Lee. They established several communities in the United States by the early 19th century. They attracted many followers, especially in New England, and became the largest and most famous sect of the 19th century. By 1840, there were approximately 6,000 "brothers and sisters" living in well-organized communities founded on the value of the community and the equality of men and women. They held all property in common, and for this reason were later often designated as a kind of "religious communist." Friedrich Engels saw in

---

Inventions and Developments Attributed to the Shakers

- The circular saw
- Clothes pins
- The cheese press
- A pea sheller
- A basket-weaving machine
- Threshing machine
- Rotating harrow
- A scale with sliding weights

"Set your hands to work and your heart on God."

Ann Lee, ca. 1780

"Everything produced in the community for its own use should be made conscientiously and well, but simple and without anything superfluous."

Joseph Meacham, ca. 1795

---

them living proof that a communistic society could be created.

   Their life in the community was marked by order, modesty, and diligence. Their faith expressed itself in the strict rules of their daily life, in the cleanliness and simplicity of their houses, and the clean-lined beauty of their handmade articles of daily use, their clothing, and their furniture. The form of their articles was rarely altered, but was constantly improved and, from the beginning, standardized. In contrast to other religious communities (such as the Amish and the Pennsylvania Dutch), the Shakers were open to technical innovation. They produced furniture, implements, and

Streets and houses in the Shaker communities were notably simple and neat, plain in style, and without ornamentation. Close to the street, the houses were usually painted white, while the barns and sheds were tones of dark red or brown.

cloth for sale. In the course of the 19th century, their products were distributed throughout the United States and even appeared at the World's Fair in Philadelphia in 1876. Because of its craftsmanship, its functionality, and its simple beauty, the furniture enjoyed general popularity.

Today the last two Shaker communities, in Maine and New Hampshire, do not accept new members and will therefore soon disappear. Still, under the rubric of "less is better," Shaker furniture has again come to be appreciated throughout the world and is currently manufactured under license by the German firm Habit and the Italian furniture manufacturer de Padova.

The Biedermeier age

The time between the Congress of Vienna and the bourgeois revolution of 1848 is known as the Biedermeier period in Germany. This era tends to be romanticized as a result of the popular idyllic pictures of Carl Spitzweg and Adrian Ludwig Richter—it is seen as an age of domesticity and modesty, bourgeois comfort and political moderation. The Biedermeier period stands in the German imagination as the last period before industrialization: a hallowed world where Nature has not yet been threatened by pollution and population explosions, where poverty and homelessness are not yet evident.

The name "Biedermeier" derives from a comic figure in the *Fliegende Blätter* (Flying Leaves);

1750 – 1850

Fir desk-cabinet with apple-wood veneer, Berlin, ca. 1800. Early Biedermeier desk-cabinets often include classical columns made of marble (as in this example), or other materials. Other models also incorporate classical architectural elements. Such secretaries were among the favorite furniture pieces of the Biedermeier period.

A magazine sofa with two drawers beneath the seat, Munich, ca. 1820. Together with a table and similarly upholstered chairs, the sofa formed the center of the middle-class living room.

1750 – 1850

Georg Friedrich Kersting (1785–1847), *Embroiderer at Window*, ca. 1814. Many of Kersting's oil paintings and watercolors of interiors depict bright, unassuming, and friendly Biedermeier rooms.

from 1855 onward, this character's name was synonymous with petty bourgeois virtue. The name was adopted, without its satiric edge, around the turn of the century for the entire period and for the rational and modest bourgeois attitude that found expression in the furniture, fashion, art, and literature of the period.

It was long believed that this style represented a pure middle-class reaction to the feudal Empire style that prevailed before 1814. Modern research indicates, however, that the Biedermeier style developed at court simultaneously with the backward-looking displays of prestige characteristic of the Empire style, and led to an objective and sober arrangement of private chambers at enlightened courts. Not until later was this "modern" style adopted by the higher

Veneer: veneers are extremely thinly peeled, sawed, or cut layers of wood that are glued onto what is normally a cheaper base wood in order to create a unified hardwood surface as inexpensively as possible. The technique of veneering has been known since antiquity, but has been commonly used only since the Renaissance. In 1817 a mechanical veneer-cutting machine that allowed industrial veneering was invented in Vienna.

circles of the courts, and only then did it become a fashion among the middle classes, which drew themselves back inside their four walls and away from politics, but which nonetheless became the most powerful class under industrialization.

Bourgeois domestic culture

The middle-class home of the period reflects utility, unpretentiousness, and comfort. The good bourgeois family turned away from elaborate fabrics and designs and similar luxuries, and valued instead a modestly simple overall impression. Rooms were decorated with harmonious arrangements of matching pairs of either furniture (chairs, settees, divans, tables) or other objects of decor. By this time, many pieces were no longer custom-made, but were standardized "ready-mades" (off the rack, as it were), that could be easily combined with each other because of their objective and restrained form. Typical pieces included, in addition to light chairs and sofas, graceful commodes, desks, end tables, book-cases, and glass display cabinets for gifts, souvenirs, or knickknack collections. As a rule, the furniture was made of light fir or pine, with a veneer of maple, cherry, or nut.

Glass cabinet of fir with birch veneer, Berlin, ca. 1825. Glass-fronted cabinets, etagères, and bookcases could be found in almost every educated middle-class home, displaying memorabilia, small gifts, books, cups, or other knickknack collections.

The Biedermeier period is often considered a typical German phenomenon, but the models for the new, simple, and utilitarian furniture had reached Germany through the internationally circulated English pattern books, and spread throughout Germany, Austria (as far as northern Italy and Hungary), Belgium, and Switzerland; Denmark developed its own classical style. The Biedermeier style begins to manifest the first results of industrialization, whose effects are also seen in the history of design—in the standardized ready-made pieces, in simplicity of form, in functionality, and in "modern" distribution methods.

1830 – 1880

1833	First child labor law enacted in England
1837	The coronation of Queen Victoria
1849	Death of Edgar Allan Poe
1859	Mexican Civil War
1860	Abraham Lincoln becomes the 16th American president
1861–65	American Civil War
1867	Alfred Nobel invents dynamite; Karl Marx, *Das Kapital*
1869	Opening of the Suez Canal
1870–71	The Franco-Prussian War
1872	Claude Monet paints *Impression soleil levant*, from which Impressionism later derives its name
1876	Philadelphia World's Fair; Alexander Graham Bell invents the telephone
1886	The Statue of Liberty, a gift from France, is erected in New York Harbor
1889	The Eiffel Tower is completed for the Paris Exposition
1890	Dismissal of Bismarck; the first underground subway is opened in London
1893	Rudolf Diesel invents the Diesel motor
1898	Marie Curie discovers radioactivity

The steam engine changes the world

In 1765 the Englishman James Watt invented the steam engine, and with it began the industrial revolution, which radically altered the life first of the people of England, and a few decades later of the rest of the world. As a result of Watt's invention, coal mining, iron and steel production, as well as machine production took on new significance: they were the preconditions for industrial mass production, a modern transportation system, and the explosive growth of the cities.

Fast new means of transportation—the railroad and steamships—were not only useful in coal min-

James Watt's steam engine, 1765. Watt mass-produced the steam engine with his partner, Matthew Boulton. The back-and-forth motion of the pistons turned gears, which in turn rotated the large flywheel. The engine found immediate use in the mining industry and in the production of pump and machine actions.

ing and iron and steel production, but they also fostered world trade. A new range of design work came into existence: railway lines, inland canals, railway stations, hotels. The growing cities gave rise to new architectural modes, such as factories, administrative buildings, and barracks for workers.

From workshop to factory

Expensive and time-consuming handwork could now be replaced by machine work, and the supply of goods for broad social classes required the inexpensive production of all sorts of consumer goods. The determining characteristic of industrial production was the division of labor: it was no longer the individual worker who crafted objects and lent them their unique form, but engineers or factory owners. In order to produce wares cheaply, the individual work cycles were further "rationalized" in the process of time. As a result, the factory worker now had to carry out only a limited number of tasks. The requirement for such a limited range of skills meant that the factory could pay lower wages, and could hire women and children, who slaved away in mines and factories under infamously terrible (sweatshop) conditions. The result was bitter poverty, terrible living conditions, and a miserable life.

By the middle of the century, however, these conditions led to worker uprisings and unrest, as well as to the formation of worker unions and parties. In 1867, Karl Marx wrote *Das Kapital*, his most influential work (and possibly the most influential social/economic tract of all time) in which he analyzed the new structures of production and society—and the misery of the proletariat.

However, toward the end of the century, within the circles of the bourgeoisie and among forward-thinking factory owners, reform movements arose

1830 – 1880

Cotton-spinning mill in Manchester, England, ca. 1855. The spinning machines were placed in long rows and powered by a steam engine via a long drive shaft. Women and children were preferred as workers as they could be paid lower wages.

Replica of the first German railway locomotive (1835) that traveled between Nuremberg and Fürth.

29

1830 – 1880

The classic Singer Sewing Machine, ca. 1871.
Isaac Singer did not invent the sewing machine—the first experiments in this direction were undertaken in France and Austria—but an earlier, almost identical model by the Frenchman Barthélemy Thimonnier arrived at the 1851 Great Exhibition in London a few days too late, and so Singer received the jury prize. His financial success was thus assured. Singer was one of the first entrepreneurs to offer time payments to private households, a shrewd and highly successful marketing approach.

The *Remington No. 1*, the first mechanical typewriter, 1876.

aimed at combatting the negative effects of industrialization—the poor living conditions of the workers, the increasing pollution, and—according to the views of the time—the badly made, overly decorated consumer commodities and fixtures typical of mass production. In particular, the English arts and crafts movement, exponents of art nouveau, the Vienna Workshops (Werkstätte), and the German Work Alliance (Werkbund) pursued these aims.

Technology and mechanization

The increasing mechanization that accompanied industrialization encompassed not only production methods, but the products themselves. The 19th century was the age of the engineer: there seemed to be no limit to the abundance of the engineer's ingenuity. By the middle of the century, the United States had taken over the leadership in this area. In 1869, the two coasts were united by the Union Pacific Railway. In 1874 the first electric streetcar rolled in New York; in the following year Thomas Edison developed the incandescent light bulb and the microphone; Isaac Merritt Singer had been producing the household sewing machine since 1851; Alexander Graham Bell exhibited a working telephone at the Philadelphia World's Fair in 1876, the same year that the first mechanical typewriter, invented by P. Remington, went into production. Even killing was mechanized: in 1835 Samuel Colt patented his revolving-breech pistol, better known eventually as the revolver.

The Pullmann car

The railroads were fitted with luxurious equipment. For the long distances traveled across the transcontinental railways, industrialist G.M. Pullmann introduced the famous Pullmann car, at once a wagon for sleeping, eating, and traveling. With well-thought-out, mechanically movable fixtures, the sleeper offered a high degree of comfort in a very small area.

Patent furniture

Meanwhile, in Europe, swivel chairs, adjustable seats, and other forms of patented furniture appeared in hair salons, doctors' examining rooms, and offices. In England, the mother country of industrialization, space-saving folding furniture was already known from ships' outfittings, and since London's Great Exhibition of 1851, there was a great deal of mechanized patent furniture. The

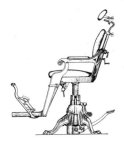

An American dentist's chair from 1879, fitted with hydraulic height adjustment.

1830 – 1880

"In the four decades between 1850 and 1890, no aspect of daily life in the United States could be taken for granted. Virtually all activities were informed by an unbridled spirit of inventiveness. This included the design of furniture. An invention demanded freedom from anxiety and courage—to allow one always to look with fresh eyes; in any era, these qualities constitute the power of the country."

Siegfried Giedion, The Power of Mechanization, *1948*

appearance, and the popularity, of these more utilitarian, engineered designs has been eclipsed in the popular imagination by the ostentatious period pieces preferred by the well-to-do Victorian consumer with an eye out for cutting a fine figure and making a fine impression.

In the United States, industrial mass production developed more consistently than anywhere else. By the middle of the 19th century, the first automatic assembly lines were in use, first in the large slaughterhouses of Cincinnati and Chicago, then in the sewing machine industry, and finally in the automobile industry. The design of the new commodities—machines and patent furniture (and

In 1875–76, Thomas Alva Edison (1847–1931) invented the phonograph, the microphone, and the incandescent light bulb. By 1878, the first electric street lamps were in place in London.

31

1830 – 1880

High-pressure steam engine, 1840, in the form of a temple. Already in the early phases of industrialization, modern machines were concealed behind historical façades. Technical devices were still mythologically presented as works of art.

A toilet bowl, Nautilus. In addition to excessive ornamentation, classical allegories and mythological references were popular devices used to glorify the nature of modern industrial products.

prime rib, or the machine for butchering to produce it)—was of a pragmatic, technical kind, lacking any sort of artistic decoration. Products like the Model T Ford were conceived for broad mass usage and often faced no real market competition; their aesthetic appearance, therefore, was of little consequence, and was accorded little consideration, at least in the beginning. Furniture for the wealthier classes was another matter altogether: among upper-class Americans, a rather conservative taste ruled, and historically oriented forms were preferred as indicators of European cultivation.

Industrial expansion and historicism

Between 1870 and 1885, a second wave of industrialization spread rapidly across the European continent, despite a great economic crisis. In fact, pressure to industrialize was increased by the demand for cheap mass-produced wares in the fast-growing cities. In Germany, the French reparation payments after the Franco-Prussian War, which persisted until approximately 1873, also led to the founding of many new factories and enterprises.

The technical advances of the 19th century resulted in new methods of production, new commodities, and new equipment with new functions. But a new aesthetic of industrial products was not initially part of the picture. For many of the new mechanical objects there was no tradition of either form or usage, leaving questions of design shrouded in uncertainty, with no historical precedence to build upon.

Around the middle of the 19th century, a backward-looking movement arose, with a search for styles with historical influences (direct or otherwise). The Romantic era (in Germany, France, and England, in particular) had already sparked a return to the forgotten sources of the Middle Ages, but now, in art and architecture and the applied arts, elements from Romanticism, the Gothic, the Renaissance, and the Baroque were seemingly arbitrarily mixed together; the result, for instance, was that even cheap machine-punched lead casings for new technical equipment were decorated with elaborate ornamentation. Furniture was outfitted with exchangeable machine-lathed decorative strips in neo-Gothic or neo-Baroque style in attempts to imitate traditional forms and handmade craftsmanship.

Prestige and display

Such excessively ornate furniture and ordinary goods were avidly sought by the generation of entrepreneurs who had become rich in the competitive struggles of the second half of the century. Financial success for them was the sole measure of social standing—and they wished to demonstrate or establish their position clearly. They quickly overthrew the plainer Biedermeier forms and replaced them with a cluttered ornamental, historical display, often with oriental influences. The self-confident middle class no longer sought to differentiate itself from the aristocracy, but rather imitated the upper class' feudal life-style and living arrangements. Wealth expressed itself directly in a richness of style and ornamentation. The apartments of the upper middle class were accordingly cluttered, the windows hung with heavy drapes, the furniture made from dark exotic woods. The pieces, heavy and oversized, stood in place, stolid and immovable. Art objects served primarily to support the decor and demonstrate the "culture" of the owner. This historicism soon filtered down through the social hierarchy, until even the lower classes were demanding ornate decor (or perhaps taste began to be dictated from above, and the lower classes had little choice but to choose from the offerings of the marketing taste

Table telephone, 1888, modern technology beneath a historical façade.

1830 – 1880

An elaborate sink from the "Athena" series from a turn-of-the-century catalog of an English plumbing fixtures firm; modern bath fixtures were built with electrical lighting in historical decor.

A living room of a well-to-do bourgeois home, ca. 1890.

1830 – 1880

World Exhibitions as Milestones of Technological and Industrial Development

1851 London: the Great Exhibition at the Crystal Palace
1854 Munich: Thonet presents the first bentwood chairs
1873 Vienna: World economic crisis ends the first era of German industrial development
1876 The Philadelphia World's Fair: the sewing machine and Shaker furniture
1884 Chicago
1889 The Paris Exposition—the Eiffel Tower draws 28 million visitors; automobile exhibit
1897 Brussels
1900 Paris—first escalator
1904 The St. Louis World's Fair coincided with the third Olympic games

makers). Patterns from various epochs circulated everywhere as models, while craft and industry delivered cheap and poorly mass-produced wares.

The Victorian era

The Victorian period in England was an epoch of economic prosperity; the Victorians looked with pride and satisfaction on their technical advances just as they regarded their colonial and economic power and the extension of their empire. The prevailing view in the design of commodities for the marketplace was that technical, practical forms were tasteless, and that the industrial origin of manufactured goods should be hidden beneath a decorative surface.

This historicism, with its oppressive and dishonest vocabulary of forms, coupled with the poor quality and lack of durability of the goods produced in such a milieu, soon became the chief target of several reform movements in Europe.

World exhibitions and international competition

The second half of the 19th century, a period of technology and mechanization, also became the age of the great world exhibitions. The growing world trade provided itself with an international marketplace where the industrial products of the leading economic nations could compete with each other. The fairs were not only showplaces of international competition but also platforms for presentations of national differences. While the exhibitions marked milestones of industrial development, they also brought to light what were false developments as well as a kind of general helplessness in questions of design, ultimately providing an arena in which the competitiveness of industrial production among the various nations par-

The Crystal Palace, designed by Joseph Paxton (1801–65) for the Great Exhibition in London, 1851, made a clear break with traditional architecture. The use of glass and iron eliminated the traditional separation of interior and exterior. Engineering techniques and new materials now determined the aesthetic of a building.

1830 – 1880

ticipating would be tested. In such a setting, historicism was increasingly perceived as an aesthetic stumbling block in international competition. Thus, Gottfried Semper criticized the Great Exhibition in London in 1851 as a "confused mixture of forms or childish dilly-dallying." He was not alone in his judgment: the London exhibition, which was supposed to be the first of its kind to show new materials and technological products from around the world and to be an expression of the industrial age, was marked by an overblown variety of ornaments, patterns, and historical style references, and was criticized from all sides. Even the London *Times* spoke of "sins against good taste."

The Eiffel Tower, designed by French engineer Alexandre Gustave Eiffel (1832–1923), was built for the Paris Exposition of 1889. Its 984-foot tower was an imposing symbol of industrial and technological development.

Michael Thonet
(1796 – 1871)

At a time when the form of most factory-produced furniture was determined by the traditions of manual labor, and factories still blindly sought to imitate handmade designs with their new power-driven lathes and bandsaws, one furniture maker succeeded in exploiting the possibilities of the new production techniques and thereby opened the door to a new, simpler furniture design. Michael Thonet, pioneer of modern furniture production, was a carpenter, inventor, and entrepreneur from the Rhineland who sought to combine handcrafted precision with modern industrial methods. He was not satisfied to employ industrial processes merely to imitate pre-industrial production, but was determined to make modern techniques into a principle of design.

Around 1830, Thonet began to experiment with ways of bending wood furniture components into curves. To this end he developed a process by which solid beech staves could be bent into round and S-shaped forms under pressure of steam. The chairs he constructed were thus ideally suited to serial factory production and, furthermore, could be easily dismantled and shipped around the world—one of the reasons for the enormous success of the firm.

Thonet's first pieces were still reminiscent of the oppressive Biedermeier style of the day, yet in contrast to the heavy, expensive furniture of the post-Franco-Prussian War boom, Thonet's furniture was sleek, light, inexpensive, and practical. The chairs attracted such attention that Thonet was invited to Vienna by Metternich, where, with the firm of Carl Leistler, he carried out several contracts for the Austrian court.

In 1849 Thonet and his five sons founded their own company in Vienna for the production of bentwood fur-

The Thonet Chair No. 14 (1859) became the model for the bentwood chair and a prototype for modern mass-produced furniture. By 1930, 50 million chairs had been manufactured—and they are still in production today. The French architect Le Corbusier stood in awe of the chair: "There is absolutely nothing more elegant, superior in concept, more precise in its construction, or more practical."

Trinkhalle, in Interlaken, Switzerland, equipped with Chair No. 14, ca. 1908. The light, practical Thonet chairs, later also known as Viennese coffeehouse chairs, were inexpensive because of their industrialized production, and thus became a staple of offices, theaters, and cafés.

niture. Soon they had contracts for cafés and public buildings. The business grew steadily, employing 42 workers by 1853. In the meantime, Thonet's sons had taken over the management and introduced the steam engine into production. The brothers set up a new factory in 1856 in a heavily forested area of the present-day Czech Republic. In the following years they continued to expand, even establishing their first foreign subsidiary in London in 1862. Their largest factory was founded in Frankenberg, Germany, in 1889. By 1900, this factory alone employed 6,000 workers who, with 20 steam engines, produced 4,000 pieces of furniture per day.

The popularity of the furniture at various world fairs as well as its success in the world market naturally led to imitation by other firms that simply appropriated the Thonet process for themselves. In the following decades, the firm underwent development typical of German family firms of the era: transformation into a stock-holding corporation, merger with a leading rival firm, wartime destruction of production facilities in the west of Germany, and nationalization of plants in the east. However, the firm survived. Today, antique Thonet furniture is displayed at international exhibitions and the much sought-after collector and museum pieces are still being produced.

How to Bend Wood

The precut beech staves are heated in pressurized steam chambers to over 100° C (212° F). The staves, which by now are fairly elastic, are placed by hand into iron molds. To prevent the wood from splitting, a thin steel band is bound tightly against the outside of the curve; this allows the wood to be bent beyond its ordinary breaking point. In the next step, the bentwood is slowly dried at 70° C (approximately 160° F) for 20 hours. Only then is it taken out of the mold, sanded, stained, and polished.

1850 – 1914

1844   Weavers uprising in Silesia

1848   March Revolution in Germany; Dante Gabriel Rossetti and others found the Pre-Raphaelite Brotherhood in England

1849   Gustave Courbet, *The Stone Breakers*

1852   The majority of the British population live in cities

1857   Jean-François Millet, *The Gleaners*

1868   Beginning of the German workers union movement

1873–76   Friedrich Nietzsche, *Untimely Reflections*

1874   First collective exhibition of Impressionist paintings in Paris; Richard Wagner, *Die Götterdämmerung*

1896   Start of the "garden city" movement in England; *Die Jugend* starts publication in Munich

1907   Foundation of the German Werkbund

Reform movements

During the second half of the 19th century, while technology celebrated its triumphs, industry and economics were growing at an ever faster rate, even if this boom was interrupted by the global economic crisis of 1873. With the growth of industry arose deplorable conditions for the working class. Educated sectors among the middle class soon made the connection between social conditions and the aesthetic and economic problems brought to light by international comparisons at the various world exhi-

Wallpaper pattern by William Morris (1834–96). As an answer to industry and large cities, mass production and historicism, Morris, like many of the reform movements, advocated a return to nature and handcraft.

Art nouveau table lamp by Peter Behrens, 1902. Art nouveau became the most important reform movement at the turn of the century. Following an English model, it replaced the forms of historicism with forms drawn from nature.

bitions: mass production certainly enabled the production of modern utensils and furniture, but the products were often covered with cheap quasi-historical or kitschy nationalistic emblems, ornaments, and decoration. These articles, mass-produced for the masses, were often poor in quality, impractical, and ill-suited to the conditions of the people for whom they were intended: in the cramped living quarters of the majority of urban dwellers, such oversized, over-decorated furniture was simply inappropriate.

A call for reform came from many camps. Supporters of socialism and of the trade union movement demanded improved living conditions and simple, inexpensive, and "honest" consumer goods for the workers. The more-educated middle class was disturbed by—next to the social problems—the ugly eclectic designs that led to an overbearing mixture of styles bearing little relation to modern industrial manufacturing. Economic and trade representatives bemoaned the reduced competitiveness of such products on the growing world market.

Thus, first in England and later in Germany, movements arose aimed not only at combating the deplorable social conditions but at reforming commercial art as well. In the face of the negative results of industrialization and the struggle against historicism, the reform groups shared similar goals, though they often differed on political, aesthetic, and economic methods. It was difficult to find consensus within individual reform

Joseph Maria Olbrich, Poster for the artist colony in Darmstadt, 1901. Darmstadt was a center of the Jugendstil, the German branch of art nouveau. Many of the artists of the movement lived in artist colonies or belonged to communal workshops.

1850 – 1914

Advertising poster for the German edition of Ebenezer Howard's *Garden Cities in View*.

"There is a danger that the present development of civilization is in the process of destroying every beauty of life ..."

William Morris

movements, and the disagreements that arose were often heated.

Reform of furniture design and of other commodities was often a facet of much more comprehensive movements seeking to improve the living and working conditions of the inhabitants of the century's expanding cities. Furniture for workers became a new field of design. In England enlightened captains of industry built the first worker settlements around 1860. In 1898 the Englishman Ebenezer Howard drew up the first plans for a so-called garden city; these were to be settlements whose green areas and small individual houses with gardens were supposed to replace the large city tenements. These English worker communities (precursors to the modern housing estates) became the model for similar reforms on the continent. In 1891 the Krupp firm built their first worker settlement; in 1909 the first German garden city was built in Dresden-Hellerau. By the turn of the century, a number of extremely different reform movements had developed, including the labor movement, the garden city movement, the nature and homeland protection movements, as well as the land, dwelling, and school reform movements.

These movements in the areas of commercial design and social reform mark the beginning of modern design history, as we defined it earlier, in that the connections among industrial manufacturing, form, function, and use began gradually to be recognized and transformed.

Pre-Raphaelites: The Pre-Raphaelite Brotherhood, founded by Dante Gabriel Rossetti and a small coterie of his friends, was a union of artists who wanted to reform English art. They demanded a return to nature as well as to clear and simple modes of composition. They preferred medieval themes. Their ideals were the Italian painters of the 15th century, the period before Raphael. The Pre-Raphaelites were an important impulse behind William Morris and the later art nouveau movement.

William Morris (1834-96) studied at Oxford between 1853 and 1855. He was the father of the arts and crafts movement and became the most important voice for the renewal of artistic handwork.

William Morris and the arts and crafts movement

The dilemma of historicism became crystal clear at the Great Exhibition of London in 1851, and it was in England that the first reaction to the prevailing trends was felt. In addition to Henry Cole, one of the organizers of the exhibition, and Gottfried Semper, the German who was living in London at the time, Owen Jones took on the problem of ornamentation in his 1856 *Grammar of Ornaments*.

Among the most significant and influential champions of a new form was artist, poet, and social critic William Morris. Unlike Cole or Jones, Morris vehemently opposed industrial mass production. Morris saw the effects of industrialization—environmental pollution, alienating work, poor-quality mass wares—as a "devilish capitalistic botch and an enemy of mankind." He became a disciple of socialism, but was no revolutionary. For him, aesthetic and social problems were inseparable, and he claimed that the answer to these problems lay in a reform of commercial art that was to return to the spirit of the Middle Ages when art and production were still closely connected to one another and artists fashioned goods that were both useful and beautiful. Morris demanded craftsmanlike consumer goods on a high aesthetic level. Against the decorative profusion of historicism, he placed natural ornaments and materials and clearly structured forms. It is not surprising that he is called one of the first serious environmental protectionists.

Cloth design by William Morris, 1876; cotton hand-printed with natural dyes.

1850 – 1914

Rush-seated chairs from the catalog of Morris & Co.

John Ruskin (1819–1900). Writer, social philosopher, art critic, and painter, member of the Pre-Raphaelites. From the middle of the century, Ruskin exerted a decisive influence on the taste of England through his writings. He attempted to address social problems by aesthetic reforms and to reform handcrafts.

The Red House built in 1859 by Philip Webb for William Morris in Kent. The house followed the design of old English country estates. The deep eaves of the tile roof and the Gothic windows create a medieval impression. Its functional elements, however, were very modern.

Title page of *Die Jugend* (Youth), Munich, 1896. The art nouveau movement in Germany derived its name from this newspaper.

Morris had studied theology at Oxford, but soon turned to painting and, along with Edward Burne-Jones and other painters, poets, and students of architecture, joined an artists' brotherhood that looked to the era predating Italian Renaissance painter Raphael for inspiration—the Pre-Raphaelites. Morris's practical design work started with the construction of the Red House, designed by his friend Philip Webb and built with the help of his friends, because he was not satisfied with the Victorian selection of furniture. From this project, the firm Morris & Co. came into existence in 1861 for the production of

solidly and tastefully produced furniture, naturally dyed cloth, handwoven rugs, painted tiles, and stained glass windows. Morris spread his artistic and social thought through publications printed, along with the works of other poets, in bibliophilic quality by his own Kelmscott Press, which he founded in 1890. Morris is well known for the type designs, page borders, and bindings of the books Kelmscott published.

The arts and crafts movement

William Morris was a friend of the art critic and philosopher John Ruskin and of the painter and illustrator Walter Crane. Their theories, as well as the practical example of their collaboration, became a model for many art guilds, including the Arts and Crafts Exhibition Society established in 1888.

With its rejection of historicism, the return to handcrafts, the weight given to art in the practice of design, and its preference for simpler, organic forms from nature, the arts and crafts movement had an important influence on the art nouveau movement, the German Werkbund, and the Bauhaus movement.

Art nouveau, an international movement

Around the turn of the century on the continent, a reform movement developed that, like the closely related arts and crafts movement, rejected historicism and sought simpler, more honestly constructed forms in the patterns of nature.

Art nouveau developed into an international movement in the years between 1895 and the First World War. In England it was called the "decorative style"; in Belgium and France, art nouveau after the furniture house of the same name; in Germany *Jugendstil* (youth style) after the magazine *Die Jugend*; in Italy, the *Stile Liberty* drew its name from the London design house Liberty which had a store on Regent Street; in Austria the designation *Sezessionsstil* was taken from the businesses, workshops, and newspapers that were promoting the new thinking in design; even Spain felt its influence, and called it *Modernista*. The cities in which the movement was most at home became the centers of art nouveau.

Arthur Mackmurdo (1851–1942), title page of the magazine *Wrens City Churches*, 1883, woodcut. Mackmurdo was a disciple of William Morris and is generally accounted one of the first art nouveau artists.

Walter Crane (1845–1915), painter, commercial artist, and illustrator, was influenced by Japanese art and the Pre-Raphaelites. As a cofounder of the arts and crafts movement, he designed wallpaper, rugs, posters, ceramics, and embroidery; he was known as an outstanding book designer.

1850 – 1914

Peter Behrens, *The Kiss*, 1898. In this colored woodcut, the hair acts as a moving ornament as well as symbolizing the fusion of the two figures.

43

1850 – 1914

> "This ornamentation arises out of the object with which it is connected. It refers to the purpose or its own method of construction. Ornamentation becomes organic to the object and refuses to be nothing more than something glued onto it."
>
> *Henry van de Velde,*
> *1901*

Henry van de Velde (1863–1957), painter, architect, and art critic, first studied painting in Antwerp and joined the artist group "Les Vingts" in Brussels in 1889. Two years later he became artistic adviser to the court of Weimar where he was director of the Commercial Art Teaching Institute from 1906 to 1914 and was cofounder of the German Werkbund. In 1917 he emigrated to Switzerland, moved back to the Netherlands from 1921 to 1947, and finally returned to Switzerland where he lived until his death. His practical and theoretical work in Belgium, Holland, and Germany made him a central figure of art nouveau.

Art nouveau, whose beginnings are usually associated with the turn of the century, had its roots in the 1880s where one finds early examples of the new forms in English prints and books, which assumed responsibility for a return to nature from the arts and crafts movement and found expression in organically flowing lines, stylized plant designs, flower stems, and tendrils. Lilies and water lilies were favored for their symbolic value; their asymmetrical shapes gave the appearance of the forms of growth found in nature.

Another development of art nouveau, particularly popular in England, was inspired by geo-

Henry van de Velde, Tobacco Shop of the Havana Company, Berlin, 1899. Van de Velde's design included architecture, shelving, chairs, and wall painting, so that the entire design worked as an organic whole. The wall painting depicts stylized smoke trails.

metrical forms drawn from Japanese art, as the Western world discovered the Far East.

The new ornamentation was quickly carried into architecture, furniture making, and all other areas of design because the goal of the art nouveau supporters was to transcend the boundary between pure and applied art. Artists were supposed to design not just "art," but jewelry, wallpaper, fabric, furniture, tableware, and more. As an answer to industrial mass wares, art nouveau strove for a comprehensive artistic reformation of all areas of life. A room was not just a room in which one placed art, but was considered a total work of art, to which ornamentation served as a linking member, not arbitrarily employed as in historicism, but organically arising from the construction and function of an object.

Belgium

Brussels early developed into a center for advanced artists and designers. The art groups *Les Vingt* and *La Libre Esthétique* boasted works by such artists as Auguste Rodin, Aubrey Beardsley, Odilon Redon, and others in the 1880s. Even the fabrics and wallpapers designed by William Morris could be found here. Moreover, the architects Henry van de Velde and Victor Horta, two of the most famous representatives of art nouveau, also belonged to the Belgian scene.

In Brussels, the ornamental principles of art nouveau were carried over into a third dimension at an early date. Horta produced the first and most significant example of art nouveau architecture. He utilized the new materials, iron beams and glass, introduced by London's Crystal Palace (1851) and the Eiffel Tower (1884–89). Horta employed the floral ornamentation of art nouveau as both a surface decoration and a constructive element. Among his most important works are the Maison du Peuple (1896–99), the Tassel House (1893), and villas Solvay (1894) and van Eetvelde (1897–1900). Using modern materials, Horta was able to construct self-supporting

Henry van de Velde, Chair, Brussels, 1898.

Victor Horta, a staircase in the Tassel House, Brussels, 1893.

Art Nouveau Journals

The Studio, London (founded 1893)
Pan, Berlin (founded 1895)
Die Jugend, Munich (founded 1896)
Simplicissimus, Munich (founded 1896)
Revue Blanche, Paris (founded 1891)
Ver Sacrum, Vienna (founded 1898)

Centers of Art Nouveau

Paris, Nancy, Brussels, Vienna, Barcelona, Glasgow, Darmstadt, Munich, Dresden, Weimar, Hagen

Emile Gallé (1846–1904), French glass and ceramic artist and founder of the School of Nancy, studied philosophy and botany in Nancy and Weimar. In 1886 Gallé established a furniture factory and enjoyed great success at the World Exposition in Paris in 1900.

Emile Gallé, glass vase with eternal autumn pattern, ca. 1900.

Hector Guimard (1867–1942), French architect and furniture designer, studied at the Ecole Nationale des Arts Décoratifs in Paris. Guimard was influenced by the English neo-Gothic and by the architecture of Victor Horta. At the turn of the century he had many commissions and became famous through his work for the Compagnie Générale du Métropolitain in 1903. After the First World War and the demise of art nouveau, he turned to architecture with standardized building elements and to building living quarters for workers. From 1938 until his death he lived in New York.

cantilevered structures to create large, bright interior spaces. Horta designed iron columns, which could be formed at will, to grow out of the ground like lily plants; together with the furniture and wall paintings, the columns formed a unified and dynamic work of art in which decoration and transparent construction were visibly melded together: the building itself became an ornament.

The younger Henry van de Velde, also a painter and architect, became more famous than Horta as a theoretician and furniture designer. Like Horta, van de Velde demanded that art be a part of design and that the shaping of a room was a total work of art. But van de Velde sought a stronger relationship between organic ornamentation and the idea of function. His theoretical comments, however, disseminated through numerous publications and lectures, reveal considerable contradictions with his actual designs. Only later in his career, with the setting up of the Villa Hohenhof for Hagen industrialist and art patron K.E. Osthaus in 1908, did van de Velde's style become more objective. He, too, was an opponent of historicism and "artistic arbitrariness," and like most of the other art nouveau artists, he was a champion of crafts, who sought reforms only against industry, while his furniture reflected the highest artistic ideals. They also reflected the highest possible prices. His role in the German Werkbund reveals this apparent contradiction.

Art nouveau in France

The most important centers of French art nouveau were Paris and Nancy. Perhaps ironically, it was the smaller provincial city of Nancy, rather than Paris, that had greater significance for the movement.

Nancy

The famous glass artists Emile Gallé and A. Daum worked in Nancy. The School of Nancy, centered in the work of Gallé, offers the clearest example of the rich floral and symbolic direction of art nouveau. Bowls, vases, and glasses imitated flowers with stem and calyx, and much of the furniture bore inscriptions meant to convey symbolic meaning.

Gallé and Daum led a glass factory which produced the most famous and delicate glass work of the art nouveau movement—only the lamps and vases of the American Louis Comfort Tiffany are better known glassworks of the style. Gallé, however, produced more than individual artistic pieces; he also produced industrially manufactured goods. In 1886 he founded a completely mechanized furniture factory with its own sawmill, workshops, steam engines, modern offices, and exhibition rooms.

The school founded by Gallé was joined by the cabinetmakers Eugène Valin and Louis Majorelle as well as by the painter, sculptor, and goldsmith Victor Prouvé. After Gallé's death, Prouvé helped attain international recognition for both the glass factory and the School of Nancy.

Paris

Unlike the other centers of art nouveau, Paris was not the site of a new school or a splinter group, nor even one of intense disagreement. Rather, the spirit of the "Belle Epoque" united the artists and allowed rich floral ornamentation

Alexandre Charpentier, music stand, ca. 1900. In its artistic consistency, the piece represents a high point of floral-organic design. The stand appears to grow out of the ground, its flowing form corresponding to musical movement.

1850 – 1914

Louis Comfort Tiffany, calyx-form glass, ca. 1900.

Hector Guimard, entrance to a Paris Metro station, ca. 1900.

47

Thomas Theodor Heine, poster for *Simplicissimus*, Munich, 1896. Heine was one of the many art nouveau graphic artists who worked for this journal.

to reach a highpoint here. Cabinetmakers like Alexandre Charpentier and Louis Majorelle worked simultaneously with expressive, but simple plant forms and with artificial and purely decorative inlaid designs.

The best-known representative of Parisian art nouveau was Hector Guimard whose entrances to the Paris Metro became the most prominent example of the union of modern technique and artistic design. The iron entrance lamps grow like plant stems up to the strong and dynamic roof beams. The roofs themselves are made of glass and resemble transparent open umbrellas. The structures no longer hide technical function behind historicizing façades, but are also clearly not functionally necessary; rather they "reconcile" with their modern ornamentation the sober technology with the brilliant metropolitan image.

Germany: The Jugendstil

The German Jugendstil also turned its back on historicism for the sake of organically flowing ornamentation, but remained less fashionable and elegant than the French art nouveau. On the contrary, the Jugendstil situated itself more be-

"It is clear to all of us that a healthy folk handcraft is only possible if it is based on simple, honest, unconditionally purpose-oriented forms."

Hermann Obrist

tween the directions of the objective-constructive and the folkart-handicraft and was more marked by reformist thought and the various theoretical formulations of the various workshops and unions based on the English model.

A significant factor in the Jugendstil movement was the desire of art patrons, princes, and entrepreneurs, who usually had contacts in England, to advance the competitiveness of German products.

August Endell, façade of the court studio, Elvira, Munich, 1896.

Richard Riemerschmid, music room chair of moor-oak and leather, designed in 1899 for the art exhibition in Dresden. In contrast to a lot of other art nouveau furniture, the chair was plain and functional. Its lightly curving diagonal side struts lend it stability and also allow the musician freedom of arm movement. © 1995 The Museum of Modern Art, New York

Richard Riemerschmid (1868–1957) exemplified the more constructivist variant of the Jugendstil. He studied painting at the Academy in Munich. Under the influence of the English arts and crafts movement, he turned to design and became a founding member of the United Workshops for Art in Craft in 1897. From 1903 he worked with the Dresden Workshops and was a co-founder of the German Werkbund in 1907. Between 1912 and 1924 he was the director of the Commercial Art School in Munich, and from 1926 to 1931 of the Werkschule in Cologne.

1850 – 1914

Munich

As in many other cities, an offshoot developed in Munich in protest against the "official" art of the Academy. The head of the movement was Hermann Obrist who, with Bernhard Pankok, Bruno Paul, August Endell, Richard Riemerschmid, and Peter Behrens, founded the United Workshops for Art in Craft in 1897. The United Workshops joined with the Dresden Workshops in 1907 to form the German Workshops for Craft Art.

In Munich, the Jugendstil also took a satiric, political side in the graphic press and in the magazines *Die Jugend* (Youth) and *Simplicissimus* (The Simpleton). Jugendstil artists were known for drafting biting caricatures, broadsides, and posters, or, like Endell, designing façades, decorations, and interior arrangements for cabarets and theaters. Endell also created the controversial, wildly turbulent façade for the court studio Elvira. Along with Obrist, Endell represented a particularly expressive variant of the Jugendstil. Still, for the development of the Jugentstil and for future developments in German design, the most important figure was Richard Riemerschmid. Riemerschmid's striving after objectivity and constructive philosophy led him to the idea of "machine furniture," which was supposed to be suited to industrial production through its form and construction.

Hermann Obrist, Embroidery, 1893. As so often happens in art nouveau, theory and practice moved at cross-currents.

49

Joseph Maria Olbrich's own house on the Mathildenhöhe in Darmstadt, 1901. The design is influenced by the traditional villa, but uses new window forms and unusual decorative elements.

Joseph Maria Olbrich (1867–1908) studied architecture at the Vienna Academy. He traveled through North Africa and Italy, and finally worked in the office of Otto Wagner in Vienna. He became a cofounder of the Viennese Secession and worked on the journal *Ver Sacrum*. Between 1899 and 1907 he built and directed the artist colony Mathildenhöhe in Darmstadt. With others, he founded the German Werkbund in 1907. In addition to his work as an architect, Olbrich designed furniture, embroidery, drinking glasses, tableware, and pottery.
Important buildings: The Secession Building in Vienna, 1898; houses on the Mathildenhöhe in Darmstadt, 1900; worker houses for the Opel Factory in Darmstadt, 1907–08; Tietz Warehouse in Düsseldorf, 1906–08.

Darmstadt

Next to art-oriented Munich, Darmstadt emerged a Jugendstil center. In 1899, the Grand Duke Ernst Ludwig of Hesse invited the cofounder of the Vienna Secession, Joseph Maria Olbrich, and Peter Behrens, one of the founders of the Munich Workshops, to Darmstadt. Their task was to develop an art colony on the Mathildenhöhe in order to inject a reform-minded momentum into Hessian industry and handiwork. Olbrich, an architect, created a complete grounds with studios, exhibition halls, and living quarters, which often

Joseph Maria Olbrich, exhibition buildings on the Mathildenhöhe, with the Wedding Tower that Olbrich erected in 1905–08 as a gift of the city of Darmstadt for the second marriage of the grand duke.

vacillated between functional construction and playful decoration. Behrens, originally an artist, had already turned to architecture and design in Munich and conceived, like van de Velde before him, of the house as a single piece of art. He designed everything first for his own house, later for others, from the roof to the tableware, and developed a considerably more objective language of design. Behrens grew well known through his activity in Darmstadt and later became one of the first modern German industrial designers.

Weimar

In 1901 Weimar was no longer the court of the muses it had been in the days of Goethe; Grand Duke Wilhelm Ernst was more Prussian power-seeker than art-loving aesthete. However, the open-minded Weimar art lover and diplomat Harry Graf Kessler engaged himself on behalf of the representatives of modern art and design. On business as well as artistic grounds, he brought van de Velde to Weimar as artistic adviser. Once there, van de Velde began to develop a more objective language of form, and his

Henry van de Velde, mahogany cabinet, Weimar, ca. 1900.

Henry van de Velde, bedroom in the "Hohenhof," Hagen, 1908. For the art patron Karl Ernst Osthaus, van de Velde designed in 1904 the Folkwang Museum in Hagen and in 1908 the Villa Hohenhof, which reflects an objective and purpose-oriented late art nouveau style.

influence on design spread throughout Germany. Between 1906 and 1914 he was director of the newly established Commercial Art Teaching Institute in Weimar, and at approximately the same time he worked for the art patron Karl Ernst Osthaus. In 1907 he co-founded the German Work Union.

Art nouveau: Between art and industry

Internationally, art nouveau was a reform movement that today must be accounted a failure. While the rebellion against historicism and poor industrial mass wares has been justifiable, art nouveau as a movement was in many respects regressive and may well have delayed the de-

Antoni Gaudí, dining room of the Casa Battló, Barcelona, 1906.
Gaudí designed the furniture as well as the overall room.

1850 – 1914

Antoni Gaudí, Church of the Holy Family, from the northeast side, Barcelona, started in 1884.

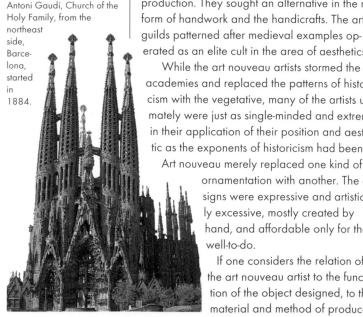

velopment of modern industrial design. Although the style created new and dynamic ornamentation, led to a new feel for space in architecture, and in design sought a more conscious relation to the materials and simpler, more honestly constructed forms, art nouveau was a step into the past. Most art nouveau designers considered themselves artists and rejected industrial mass production. They sought an alternative in the reform of handwork and the handicrafts. The art guilds patterned after medieval examples operated as an elite cult in the area of aesthetics.

While the art nouveau artists stormed the old academies and replaced the patterns of historicism with the vegetative, many of the artists ultimately were just as single-minded and extreme in their application of their position and aesthetic as the exponents of historicism had been. Art nouveau merely replaced one kind of ornamentation with another. The designs were expressive and artistically excessive, mostly created by hand, and affordable only for the well-to-do.

If one considers the relation of the art nouveau artist to the function of the object designed, to the material and method of production (hand or factory work), and even to the variety of designs (rich floral or simple geometric), it is difficult to classify many of them.

The only truly memorable representative of Spanish art nouveau was Antoni Gaudí of Barcelona. Gaudí's masterpiece, the church La Sagrada Familia, is a monumental example of artistic individuality and revolutionary form, but his achievement has little in common with any movements for reform in modern architecture and design. Even within the scope of art nouveau itself, Gaudí is considered something of an anomaly. His buildings were exceptionally dynamic, modern, and strongly colored, but the strict Catholic Catalanian drew largely from the Gothic or the Moorish, which he sculpted into Expressionistic forms.

The Italian Carlo Bugatti is also generally regarded as a "special case" in art nouveau. Bugatti's works are extreme examples of the already artistically extravagant. His furniture assumed completely new and astounding shapes and was decorated with ornaments from oriental odds and ends with Asian lettering executed in unusual materials such as copper, ivory, or vellum. And, like so much of the output of the art nouveau movement, his pieces were individually finished for Bugatti's wealthy patrons.

These two outsiders—Gaudí and Bugatti—highlight the problems of art nouveau: as new and provocative as the style was, around 1910 it virtually disappeared. The First World War and the revolutionary movements of the interwar period marked the definitive end of the movement. What survived, however, was the will to reform, and this found expression, perhaps inevitably, almost exclusively in a positive turn toward industry.

Antoni Gaudí (1852–1926) studied architecture and from 1878 constructed buildings with oriental elements. He was a strong exponent of unity of architecture and interior design, and stamped Catalanian art nouveau with so-called *Modernismo*. His controversial architectural style brought him considerable fame.

Major works: Church of the Holy Family (La Sagrada Familia), begun 1884; Casa Mila, 1905–07; Casa Battló, 1906; the palace and park Güell, 1886–89 and 1900–14. All these buildings are in or around Barcelona.

1850 – 1914

Carlo Bugatti, lady's desk with chair, Turin, 1902. The surfaces of the furniture are covered entirely with vellum and trimmed with copper.

1883 Friedrich Nietzsche, *Thus Spake Zarathustra*

1889 World Exhibition in Paris, Eiffel Tower

1890 Paul Cézanne, *The Card Players*

1898 Dresden Workshop for the Handicrafts

1901 Frank Lloyd Wright, "The Art and Craft of the Machine"

1903 The Wright brothers made the first manned motorized flight

1904 First garden city in England; subway in New York

1905 Artist union "Brücke" (The Bridge)

1906 Pablo Picasso, *Les Demoiselles d'Avignon*

1907 Foundation of German Werkbund; Peter Behrens takes over product design at AEG

1908 Adolf Loos, *Ornament and Crime*

1913 Fagus Works by Walter Gropius

1914 Outbreak of the First World War

1890 – 1914

The road to modernism

While art nouveau may have been backward-looking, extravagant, and luxury-oriented, it was nonetheless infused with a revolutionary desire based on a deep understanding that the problems of industrialization could not be solved by nothing more than a "flight back to nature." Furthermore, art nouveau by no means dictated a single style. While most people associate the style with rich floral patterns and expensive luxury furniture, it was just as strongly characterized by objective and geometric forms, stripped of all ornamentation.

Individual architects and designers became pioneers of the modern through their designs, their methods, their theoretical considerations on the functionality of objects, or their attitude toward industry. In this early phase, the connection with architecture and architectural methods was important for the breakthrough of modern design.

Representatives of art nouveau, such as Henry van de Velde, found an objective formal expression in the course of time, or they devoted themselves completely to new challenges in industry. An example of an artist following the latter course is Peter Behrens. Within the reform movements and institutions such as the German Werkbund, ardent discussions arose over the role of the artist and attitudes to industrial mass production, which everyone realized could no longer be ignored.

Mackintosh and the Glasgow School of Art

New objective forms had already come into existence on the periphery of the art nouveau movement in Great Britain, in the Scottish harbor city

Charles Rennie Mackintosh, chair for the bedroom of Hill House in Helensburgh, 1903. Reproduction by Cassina.

of Glasgow. Here in the 1890s, the Glasgow School of Art, a group of architects and artists influenced by an influx of Japanese art and the aesthetics it suggested, developed a new style. They used ornament sparingly and, with the exception of a few pastel tones, preferred black and white—a preference that was to become a hallmark of the modern. The chief figure of the group was Charles Rennie Mackintosh, whose geometric forms and shallow boardlike constructions with graceful horizontals and verticals established the direction for other precursors of the modern. Mackintosh himself was better known on the continent than in England. In Vienna in particular, he was respected and admired as a model for modern designing at the Eighth Secessionist Exhibit in 1900.

Charles Rennie Mackintosh, library wing of the Glasgow School of Art, 1907–09. The functional boxlike construction became a landmark for the coming functional understanding of architecture and design.

1890 – 1914

Vienna at the turn of the century
Another secession—that is, a splintering off from the mainstream of the art nouveau movement into a somewhat different direction, with different theories and principles—developed in Vienna. The Viennese style, like other art nouveau styles, was in opposition to the traditional academies and historicism and was based on the concept of the totality of a work of art and of reform of handicrafts. However, largely through the influence of Mackintosh, a clear formal language developed, marked by rectangularity and straight lines. The founders of the Secession were Gustav Klimt, Koloman Moser, and the nearly sixty-year-old architect Otto Wagner.

Wagner, often called the father of the Vienna Modern, was strictly classical in his orientation; for him, to turn to an objective and modern form represented no real break at all. His furniture designs were as severe as those of the Bauhaus. His major work, the Vienna Postal Savings Bank, is a striking example of the new style. The main

Charles Rennie Mackintosh's chair, from 1897, is still caught in art nouveau, with clear oriental elements.

Charles Rennie Mackintosh (1868–1928), architect and artist, studied at the Glasgow School of Art and was influenced by the aesthetics of the English Gothic and the Far East. He designed buildings, furniture, and cloth, among other things, and together with J. Herbert MacNair and Margaret and Frances Macdonald was one of the dominant forces behind the development of modern design. His entries caused a stir at the Eighth Secessionist Exhibit and influenced the Vienna Workshop, Hermann Muthesius, and the German Werkbund. After 1923, Mackintosh gave himself over entirely to painting. His furniture pieces are today considered as "modern classics" and are reproduced by the Firma Cassina. *Important architectural works*: the buildings of the Glasgow School of Art, 1897–1909; Hill House, Helensburgh, 1903; the country estate house Windy Hill, Kilmacolm, 1900.

hall is built of iron beams with a high, lightly arched glass roof. The room is functionally designed, bright, with no unnecessary decoration. Both the construction of the building and the modern materials used remain visible, from hot air vents to the aluminum sheathing on the columns; not even the rivet heads on the iron beams are concealed.

> "Ornament is a waste of the energy of labor, and therefore a waste of health. ... Today it also means squandered material, and squandered capital. ... The modern person, the person with modern nerves, does not need ornament, on the contrary, he detests it."
>
> *Adolf Loos, Ornament and Crime, 1908*

Wagner's student Josef Hoffmann called on an equally objective, geometric formal language in architecture and design. One of his major works, the Purkensdorfer Sanatorium, built in 1903–06, was topped with a modern flat roof. The consumer goods he designed still look "modern" today. In 1903 out of the Secession rose the Vienna Workshop, founded by Hoffmann and Moser, but in the 1920s the Workshop increasingly strayed in the direction of a luxurious handicrafts workshop. Another member of the circle of the early Vienna

Otto Wagner, Postal Savings Bank, Vienna, Main Hall, 1906.

1890 – 1914

Modern was Adolf Loos, who, however, was an opponent of the Vienna Workshop. Loos went well beyond the mere reduction of decor to reject ornamentation absolutely; in his numerous publications he demanded purely functional styling. Thus, in Vienna, the Jugendstil had been overwhelmed and the objective designs of Hoffmann and Moser provided an important impetus for the German Werkbund and the Bauhaus movement.

In the United States, as already mentioned, the prevailing preference for a "cultivated" European style was nonetheless paralleled by a growing movement in the direction of a pragmatism oriented toward necessity and technical feasibility. Here, "modern" signified industrial production.

Otto Wagner, armchair from the Vienna Postal Savings Bank, beechwood with aluminum fittings, 1906. Wagner also designed the interior of the bank—the simple cubistic stools in the Hall, the bentwood chairs (built by Thonet) in the offices.

1890 – 1914

"Form follows function"

Chicago, the key location for heavy industry and steel production and a major processing center for grain and cattle from the Midwest, became a center of the "early modern." It was in Chicago's

Joseph Hoffmann (1870–1956), student and colleague of Otto Wagner. With Wagner, Koloman Moser, and Gustav Klimt, Hoffmann founded the Secession. In 1903, along with Moser and Fritz Würndorfer, he also established the Vienna Workshop. Hoffmann resigned from the Secession in 1905 and founded the Austrian Werkbund in 1912.
Important architectural works: Villa for Koloman Moser, Vienna, 1901–04; Sanatorium Purkersdorf, 1903–06; Palais Stoclet, Brussels, 1905–11; various private houses, including that of the painter Ferdinand Hadler, Geneva, 1913.

Adolf Loos (1870–1933), architect and theoretician, studied 1890–93 at the Technical Academy in Dresden, after which he spent several years in the United States. Afterward he worked as an architect in Vienna, and from 1923 to 1927 in France. Loos was an advocate of functional form and an ardent opponent of the decorative art nouveau. In 1908 his famous essay *Ornament and Crime* was published.
Important architectural works: Café Museum, 1900; Kärntner Bar, 1908; Steiner House, 1910 (all in Vienna); the Tristran Tzara House, Paris, 1926.

Otto Wagner (1841–1918) studied architecture in Vienna and Berlin and taught from 1894 to 1912 at the Art Academy in Vienna. He was among the cofounders of the Vienna Secession.
Important architectural works: rental houses on the Vienna Row, 1898–99; buildings for the city streetcar line, 1894–97; Postal Savings Bank, Vienna, 1904–06.

Louis H. Sullivan, The Pirie Scott Department Store, Chicago, 1899–1904. Steel frame construction covered with white terra cotta. The display windows on the ground floor were framed in richly ornate cast iron moldings, but their clear integration in the façade, with its new triple-partitioned "Chicago windows," points the way toward modern functional architecture.

famous slaughterhouses that the first assembly lines were installed.

In 1900, Chicago had a population of 1.7 million people and was situated at a crossroads of the continent, connected to much of the country by rail, and to the Great Lakes region by the Erie Canal. Three factors favored the construction of skyscrapers: the destructive fire of 1871, which decimated large areas of the city; the technical possibility of steel skeleton construction; and the high price of land.

The most important representative of the new method of construction was Louis H. Sullivan. Sullivan is considered by many the father of modern architecture and was an early functionalist theoretician. It is from Sullivan that we have the much misunderstood, but often quoted, statement that "form follows function." From this basic concept, the representatives of functionalism—from the German Werkbund to the Bauhaus and the School of Design in Ulm to the 1970s—have drawn their body of principles.

Frank Lloyd Wright

Frank Lloyd Wright, a colleague of Sullivan, set himself up independently and developed a new understanding of architecture and design. To most

Frank Lloyd Wright, an office in the Kauffman Department Store, Chicago.

Americans, his name is synonymous with a shift toward modern American architecture and design. Like others, he considered the house an artistic whole and designed the interiors as well as the exteriors for his customers. Using the fireplace as a center point, Wright worked outward to the perimeter and created an open, asymmetrical series of rooms wholly along functional lines of sight.

The house, for Wright, was organically embedded in nature, closed to the street and open to the landscape. Horizontal cornices and wide-eaved flat roofs established a connection with the surrounding space. For these effects, Wright was one of the first to employ a reinforced steel construction.

The furniture—built in, if possible, or free standing—carried on the horizontal theme of the architecture and was constructed with severe geometry from simple surfaces (boards) and right-angled strips. For Wright, the openness of the interior and the simplicity of the materials were an expression of democracy and individuality. Wright was in fact a preacher who spread his convictions through lectures and publications. In his most famous essay, "The Art and Craft of the Machine," he admitted, at least in theory, the possibility of machine production. A portfolio of Wright's completed works, together with an exhibition, was to have a

Frank Lloyd Wright (1867–1959) designed over 800 buildings. He was clearly one of the most important architects of the 20th century. After studying engineering, Wright worked with Louis Sullivan in Chicago, and later on his own. Wright developed the modern, natural "prairie house," combined simple and natural materials with modern building materials—for example, glass and concrete with wood and stone. After 1910, he became the single most important force in the modern style.
Most important buildings: Larkin Building (office building), Buffalo, New York, 1904; Robie House, Chicago, 1907–09; Coonly House, Riverside, Illinois, 1907–11; House Fallingwater, Bear Run, Pennsylvania, 1936; Guggenheim Museum, New York, 1943–59.

1890 – 1914

Frank Lloyd Wright, Oak Park House, Oak Park, Illinois.

"Only through stand-ardization, which must be understood to be the result of healthy con-centration, can we find the way back to a uni-versally valid and sure taste."

Hermann Muthesius, 1914

marked influence on the course of European modernism: Gropius, Mies van der Rohe, Behrens.

The German Werkbund

In Germany it was primarily the Werkbund that marked the passing of the Jugendstil and the tran-sition to modern industrial design. The Werkbund was established in Munich in 1907 by a group of artists, architects, businessmen, and public figures. Its model was the English Arts and Crafts Society, but there was an important difference: the Werk-bund explicitly took into account the conditions of modern industrial production. It was not bent on turning back the clock. The Werkbund was not inherently antagonistic to machine production, but rather sought reform of industry. In its own words, its goal was "to en-able industrial work by the coopera-tion of art, industry, and handcrafts."

Among the founding members were Hermann Muthesius, Henry van de Velde, Peter Behrens, Karl Ernst Osthaus, and the liberal politicians Friedrich Naumann and Karl Schmidt, director of the Dresden Workshop, all of whom had already come out in favor of industrial mass production at their 1906 exhibition.

Karl Arnold, caricatures of the Werkbund debate of 1914 in *Simplicissimus*.

"So long as there are still artists in the Werk-bund, and so long as they still have influence on its course of action, they will protest against every proposal for an artistic canon or standardization."

Henry van de Velde, 1914

The Werkbund peaked with its famous 1914 exhibition in Cologne. In addition to standardized furniture and household objects, the exhibition offered sleeping-car interiors and a model steel and glass factory constructed by Walter Gropius.

In the same year, the longstanding argument in the Werkbund over the issue of standardization also peaked. Hermann Muthesius held that it was only through standardization of design that one could create usable industrial forms—inexpensive mass-produced products with a long lifespan. Van de Velde, on the other hand, defended the individuality of the artist's design work. This heated debate was suspended, at least for the time being, by the First World War.

After the war, under the influence of increasing social problems, attention was focused primarily on living quarters and inexpensive household fittings for the working class. The highpoint of this effort was the famous 1927 Werkbund Exhibition in Stuttgart. The show became an international forum of representatives of the modern and the

Walter Gropius and Adolf Meyer, model factory (south side) for the Werkbund Exhibition in Cologne, 1914.

1890 – 1914

Poster of the 1914 Werkbund Exhibition in Cologne

"New Bau" movement. However, within the Werkbund, opinions differed; conservatives finally went so far as to welcome the premature closure of the argument imposed by the National Socialists.

After World War II the Werkbund was reestablished. It still exists today, but has never regained the prominence that it once boasted. Along with the Bauhaus movement, the Werkbund belongs to those institutions that strongly influenced the development of modern design.

Richard Riemerschmid, machine-made chair, ca. 1906.

Peter Behrens, ca. 1912.

At the end of the 19th century, the electrical industry was experiencing explosive growth and developing into an economic sector of the future. By 1907, the AEG, founded in 1883 by Emil Rathenau, was already one of the world's leading electronic companies, along with General Electric, Westinghouse, and Siemens. The AEG produced generators, turbines, transformers, and electric motors for industry, but also manufactured increasing numbers of household electrical items: light bulbs, fans, clocks, water heaters, air humidifiers, heaters, and more.

From its earliest days, the AEG—a German company—operated according to the American model, with the latest machinery and rationalized methods of organization and production. The quickly growing firm established subsidiaries and holding companies. In 1910 the AEG had over 10,000 employees. Deals were cut with international competitors to divide the world market—what has

Peter Behrens, Cover design for a fan prospectus, ca. 1908.

"It is precisely in electrical technology that it is important not to mask forms behind decorative additions, but because the technology is a completely new area, to find forms that represent the new character of the technology."

Peter Behrens, 1910

been described as an almost "fairy-tale-like development."

The firm wanted to document its modern, forward-thinking image: it planned to use contemporary, well-designed products to contradict the negative reputation of German industrial production, as well as to overcome any residual fears people may have had of physical contact with the new equipment. For these reasons, Rathenau engaged Peter Behrens in 1907 as artistic adviser.

At that time, Behrens was already known as a cofounder of the Munich Workshop and of the artist colony in Darmstadt. From 1903 to 1907, he was director of the Düsseldorf School of Industrial Arts and in his various work, ranging from graphic arts to architecture, he had already distanced himself from art nouveau and found his way to objective and functional forms. In 1906 he was hired to create advertising material for the AEG, and in 1907 he assumed responsibility for design in all areas of the firm.

Between 1907 and 1914, Behrens completely revolutionized the company's image. He designed catalogs, price lists, and electrical equipment as well as worker apartments, fair booths, and factory build-

> "It is agreed, we refuse to duplicate handmade works, historical style forms, and other materials for production."
> *Peter Behrens, 1907*

ings—everything to appeal to the customer, but with (or precisely because of) his emphatic use of objective and functional form. Behrens strived to achieve "an inner connection between art and industry for all machine-made objects," free from superfluous flourishes and ornamentation.

The evolution of a logo. *Left to right*: From the ornate, barely legible historical design of 1896, to art nouveau, through two more modern permutations, and finally the stark, clear version designed by Peter Behrens, which AEG adopted for its logo.

With its objective, modern language of design and high artistic ideals, the AEG, as a representative of a new industry, wanted to establish a respectable reputation in the cultural arena. In everything from letterhead designs to production facilities, it recognized the importance of a firm's image for making a profit. Through Behrens's work, the AEG became the first firm in the world with a total "corporate identity"—a precedent that would have no successors for a long time to come.

Peter Behrens, AEG Turbine Hall, Berlin, 1909. The corner pillars and roof construction are reminiscent of classical motifs, but the entire hall is a self-supporting structure made of steel beams with glass surfaces. The structure remains visible.

Corporate Identity (CI): The uniform image of a firm, from an intrinsic and extrinsic perspective, intended to clearly distinguish the firm from its competition and to give it instant recognizability. The CI incorporates the design of all products, buildings, and means of communication—e.g., company magazines, advertisements, letterhead. It might even dictate the design of uniform clothing (or determination of a dress code) and social and behavioral norms toward customers. A related term is *corporate culture* (CC), which refers to the efforts of a firm to create a respected cultural image, for example, by sponsoring cultural events and social benefits for employees.

1900	Sigmund Freud, *The Interpretation of Dreams*
1909	Filippo Tommaso Marinetti, *First Futurist Manifesto*
1913	Henry Ford sets up the first automobile assembly line in Detroit
1914	Beginning of World War I
1916	Albert Einstein, *Theory of General Relativity*
1917	October Revolution in Russia
1918	End of World War I
1919	Bauhaus Manifesto
1920	Women granted the vote in the United States
1924	Death of Lenin; Charlie Chaplin, *The Gold Rush*
1925	First television demonstration in Germany and England; Exposition des Arts Décoratifs et Industriels Modernes in Paris
1926	Fritz Lang, *Metropolis*
1929	The Wall Street crash marks the beginning of the Great Depression
1933	Nazi takeover in Germany; Hitler becomes chancellor; end of prohibition in the United States
1939	Germany invades Poland; start of World War II

1915 – 1933

The period between the two world wars was marked by radical economic and social changes in all the industrial nations. Industrialization had not only brought about mass production of goods but also established a capitalist society with a large working class. The struggle for world markets had driven the industrial and colonial powers into the First World War, in the course of which socialist revolutions had erupted in Russia (1917) and in Germany (1918). The economic and political importance of industrial design had already become clear in the 19th century, and along with William Morris, many hoped to aid social reform through the intelligent design of goods for the masses. Through the Russian Revolution, which was supposed to bring about a new classless society for both manual laborers and intellectuals, art and technology were also to be reconciled. Art itself was no longer to be subdivided into pure versus applied; rather, the artist, as universal creator, was to act as a reforming and educating agent.

In a world dominated by technology, the artists of the avant-garde movement in particular saw new paths for art, and with them, the possibility of social transformation. A further idealization of technology as well as an abstraction of form were pursued by the cubists and the futurists. A few Italian futurists went so far as to glorify the war for the beauty of its technology. In the Russian movements of suprematism and constructivism, both the technique of

Vladimir Tatlin, *Monument for the Third International,* 1920 (never built). The model for the tower is Tatlin's masterwork. The spiral became the symbol of the "optimum projection" of the revolutionary movement, the development and liberation of mankind.

construction and the innate properties of the raw materials were counted among the most important factors in product design.

In Russia, Wassily Kandinsky's insistence on the liberation of art from its traditional representational function was as revolutionary as the political upheavals. The avant-garde artists celebrated a dynamic aesthetic of the Age of the Machine, reduced to nonobjective forms. The artists were active in the most varied areas of endeavor: they designed posters, book covers, new typefaces, furniture, and other utility items. They threw themselves into utopian architectural and city planning projects. The modernist ideas of the constructivist school in particular influenced the De Stijl ("The Style") movement in the Netherlands and the Bauhaus school in Germany. From the realm of art itself came the impetus for a functional aesthetic whose simple geometric forms and a color scheme reduced to black, gray, white, and the primaries still characterize our understanding of modern design today.

Many artists of the Russian avant-garde, such as Vladimir Tatlin, Kasimir Malevich, Alexander Rodchenko and El Lissitzky, understood their work to be in the service of a new society. They produced newspapers, book covers, and posters, as well as street and theater decoration as propaganda for the Soviet government. In addition they designed utility goods, clothing and furniture which, through a high degree of standard-

El Lissitzky, *Tatlin at Work on the Monument for the Third International*, 1921–22, collage. For the avant-garde artists of the 1920s, a pair of compasses was one of the insignia of modern art. The artist was to be an art engineer.

1915 – 1933

Theo van Doesburg and Cornelis van Eesteren, *Architectural Proposal*, 1923. Apart from the early modern designs of the American architect Frank Lloyd Wright, the new artistic directions of cubism, futurism, suprematism, and constructivism influenced the architecture of the Dutch De Stijl group.

Vladimir Tatlin and N. Rogoshin, Model for a chair, 1929.

1915 – 1933

"Today's furniture factories pay no attention at all to the needs of the human body when they design pieces of furniture. They are only interested in the external appearance. The human being is, however, an organic unity consisting of skeleton, nerves, and muscles. As a result, it is absolutely necessary for a chair to have springs.«
Vladimir Tatlin, 1929

Vladimir Tatlin, Proposal for men's clothing, 1923.

Vladimir Tatlin and Alexei Sotnikov, Drinking vessel for small children, 1930.

ization, were especially suited to the still primitive Russian mass-production facilities. Through simple, mass-produced goods it was imagined that the living standards of the population were to be greatly improved. However, although the design of goods had to meet the requirements of industrialized production as well as the availability of raw materials, the actual designs tended to spring equally from the abstract geometrical idiom of constructivism and the artists' sheer desire for creative expression.

Vladimir Tatlin: "The artist as a life-style organizer"

Constructivism defined itself as a culture of materials. It was in this sense that Vladimir Tatlin introduced the term in 1913. Tatlin was the first sculptor who actively devoted himself to experimentation with nontraditional materials and incorporated their properties and construction characteristics as artistic elements in his sculptures and reliefs. In the 1920s he prepared a model for the Monument for the Third International and oriented his work increasingly to the service of daily life. El Lissitzky and Alexander Rodchenko also demanded an applied art in place of a pure aesthetic. In this, all three separated themselves from other Russian avant-garde artists such as Naum Gabo, Anton Pevsner, and Wassily Kandinsky who emphasized purely intellectual and spiritual artistic concerns. Tatlin, however, was a pragmatist even among the constructivists. Like the other constructivists, he insisted on a correspondence between the method of working and the materials used, and the object created, but he rejected the constructivist axioms of the straight line and the right angle, opting instead for the curved line in both art and practical design—his emphasis was clearly on rounded forms that suited the human body. Following these principles, he devised not only theater sets and costumes, but also clothing, furniture, and a heating stove that were meant to be practical, inexpensive, and comfortable.

El Lissitzky

One of the most versatile artists of the Russian avant-garde, El Lissitzky also held the principles of modern technology to be the determining factor in artistic perception and creation. His Proun lithographs apply the visionary formal idioms of Malevich to architectural designs for

El Lissitzky, *Poster for the Pelikan Corporation,* Hanover, 1924. Lissitzky was one of the outstanding typographers and poster artists of the 20th century. He produced both propaganda and commercial posters.

1915 – 1933

El Lissitzky, *Schlagt die Weissen mit dem roten Keil* (Beat the Whites with the Red Wedge), 1920, poster.

Alexander Rodchenko, interior of a worker-club for the Soviet Union's pavilion at the Exposition des Arts Décoratifs 1925 in Paris.

a new city. In addition, he experimented with photography, created book covers and furniture, and laid out the Soviet pavilions at international fairs such as the "Presse" in Cologne (1928) and the Health Exhibition in Dresden (1930). Through his stay in Berlin and his contact with the world outside the Soviet Union, he spread the principles of constructivism and established

Constantin Roschdestvenski, Cup and saucer with suprematist decoration. Lomonossov Porcelain Factory, Leningrad

connections with the De Stijl group, the Bauhaus movement, and the Dadaists.

Porcelain and textiles

Most Soviet artists worked or taught at the "Higher State Artistic-Technical Workplace" (WCHUTEMAS) or, after 1927, at the "Higher State Artistic-Technical Institute" (WCHUTEIN) in Moscow, which had divisions for working in metal, wood, fabric, and ceramic. The main fields of application for early mass production were the porcelain and textile industries, which because of their mass distribution clearly offered the possibility to carry propagandistic messages via crockery and fabrics. Immediately after the 1917 Revolution the former Imperial Porcelain Manufacturer was reconstructed, under the new name, "State Porcelain Manufacturer," and after 1925, "Lomonossov Porcelain Factory," was also reopened, which gave young artists the opportunity to gain experience in production. S. Chechonin was their artistic supervisor from 1918 to 1923 and from 1925 to 1927. At this time, Wassily Kandinsky, Vladimir Lebedev, Nicolai Mikhailovich Sujetin, and Kasimir Malevich worked in the artistic division. Much of the china carried suprematist mottoes, or had, after the instatement of the "New Economic Politics" of 1921 and increasingly until the end of the 1920s, the Revolution as a theme.

Mikhail Adamovich, plate with menu, portrait of Lenin and the propaganda message: "Whoever does not work should not eat," 1923. Commemorative pottery bore revolutionary slogans or images, or the Soviet symbol: the hammer and the sickle.

Fabric design

The textile industry was also expected to take on political work, by providing a vehicle for communicating the message of the Revolution. The older generation of textile artists such as Olga Rosanova, Varvarya Stepanova, Ljubov Popova,

L. J. Raizer, *Mechanization of
the Red Army*, silk fabric
design, 1933

and Alexander Rodchenko had already favored
the abstract geometry of constructivism and suprematism as aesthetic signs for an international and
classless industrial brotherhood. Later, toward the
end of the 1920s, especially with the beginning
of Stalin's forced industrialization, young textile
designers including L. J. Raizer and Marya Nazarevskaya strove for a stronger proletarianization of
art. Just as they had turned against bourgeois
floral patterns, they now condemned as "formal-
istic" the geometry of constructivism, and sought
new, concrete-figurative ornaments that were
supposed to spread the program of socialism
among the uncultured workers and builders. The
old folk-art patterns were replaced with rows of
machines and tractors and brigades of workers.
An intense controversy developed, however,
among the sketch artists over the production of
these highly figured patterns. Nobody seemed
ready or willing to accept the folksy tractors and
harvesters as pattern materials, so on the command of the People's Commissar in 1933, the
fabrics were no longer produced.

1915 – 1933

A creative internationale
The industrial products of the avant-garde were a
real propaganda instrument of the Soviet regime,
and were shown at the "First Russian Arts Exhibition" in 1922 in Berlin, the "International Exposition of Decorative Arts" in 1925 in Paris, and
other international exhibitions. Moreover, many

Marya Nazarevskaya, *Red
Army Soldiers in the Cotton
Fields,* silk fabric design, 1932.

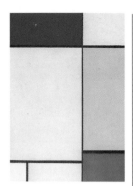

Piet Mondrian, *Composition*, ca. 1922, oil on canvas. In 1917 Mondrian formulated his "theory of plasticism," according to which art must be completely abstract. As compositional elements, only horizontal and vertical lines may be used. Colors are limited to the primaries (red, blue, and yellow), along with black, white, and grey.

Gerrit Rietveld and employees in front of his workshop in Utrecht, 1918. Rietveld is sitting on the prototype of the later Red and Blue Chair.

Gerrit Rietveld, *Side table of Lacquered Wood*, 1922-23. Modern reproduction by the Cassina firm, Milan.

1915 – 1933

pieces from the Lomonossov Factory were exported to the West, where they were certainly *not* acquired by the working masses, but, on the contrary, landed in the hands of wealthy collectors.

The Netherlands: De Stijl (1917–31)

The result of all this activity was that the Russian avant-garde provided an important impulse for architecture and modern design in the West. In interaction with Russian constructivism as well as other abstract movements, a radical new movement arose in the Netherlands which absolutely rejected every attempt to reproduce nature in art, and instead posited painting, for example, as an autonomous interworking of form, surface, and color. The movement sought to eliminate all

"The life of cultured people today has less and less to do with the abstract idea."

Piet Mondrian, in De Stijl No. 1, 1917

traces of the emotional and personal in art and rigorously held art to axiomatic and constructivist principles.

In 1917 Theo van Doesburg established a new journal in Leyden. Known simply as *De Stijl*, the magazine provided a forum for a group of painters, architects, and sculptors to publish their theories and manifestos presenting a new and radically modern philosophy of art. Among the coworkers of the journal and original members on the De Stijl group were, besides van Doesburg, the painters Piet Mondrian, Bart van der Leck, and Vilmos Huszár; the architects Jacobus J. Oud, Jan Wils, and Robert van't Hoff; the sculptor Georges van Vantongerloo; and the poet Wim Kok. In 1918 the group was joined by Gerrit Rietveld, and in 1922 by Cornelis van Eesteren. The De Stijl group, however, was by no means a closed circle; it included the constructivist El Lissitzky, the futurist Gino Severini, as well as representatives of the German Dada scene, such as Hans Arp, Hugo Ball, and Kurt Schwitters.

For the artists of De Stijl, pure abstraction and strict geometrical arrangement provided the true formal aesthetic for a modern technical and industrial society. And because they deemed art to be in the vanguard of society, the ideal of pure formalism was to be carried into all areas of life in order to create a new, harmonious order independent of nature. This rigorous formal simplicity and the rejection of decorative ornamentation were rooted in the puritanism of Dutch Calvinist society: the aspirations of De Stijl were always tinged by elements of protestant iconoclasm. And now this formal asceticism was to carry forward the program of the modern and serve the ideals of functionalism and the technical requirements of industrial production as well. Thus, the traditional bourgeois ethos came full circle to meet the avant-garde utopia.

Furniture design

The forms were also to be simplified to their basic, eternal elements in furniture design. Rietveld's furniture reflected De Stijl principles as if they constituted a manifesto. His famous Red and Blue

Piet Mondrian (1872–1944), had moved from post-Impressionism and cubism to abstract art. Cofounder of the De Stijl movement, he broke with van Doesburg in 1925, but renewed their friendship in 1929 and in 1931 became a member of van Doesburg's new artist group, Abstraction-Creation.

Theo van Doesburg (1883–1931), a publicist and critic, was the theoretician of the group. He propagated the ideas of De Stijl through publications and travels in Europe, and established contact with the Bauhaus school and the Russian constructivists.

1915 – 1933

Gerrit Thomas Rietveld (1888–1964), influenced by Frank Lloyd Wright, designed his own furniture from 1900 on. A member of the De Stijl group since 1918, in the course of the 20th century he turned to architecture and was cofounder of the Congrès International de l'Architecture Moderne (CIAM) in 1928.

Jacobus Johannes Pieter Oud (1890–1963), architect, was influenced by H. P. Berlage and Frank Lloyd Wright. He was cofounder of De Stijl and after 1918, the City Architect of Rotterdam. In 1921 he broke with van Doesburg, and in 1922 with Mondrian. He maintained contact with the Bauhaus movement and participated with great success in the International Building Exhibition in Stuttgart in 1927. He turned down several posts at important universities.

1915 – 1933

Chair, consisting merely of several pieces of wood as framing elements and two boards that serve as seat and backrest, was eminently suited to machine production. The constructivist element is also apparent in the clear primary colors. The effect of the whole is unmistakably reminiscent of Mondrian's paintings. Thus, the chair, at once a totally practical household item as well as a work of art,

"Our chairs, tables, and closets as well as other appropriated objects are the 'abstract-real' sculptures of our future interiors."

Theo van Doesburg about Rietveld's furniture design

combined De Stijl's aesthetic ideals of form with the functional and social requirements of mass production. The distinction between art and life becomes moot. Rietveld's later designs never passed beyond the prototype stage into production, although all were

Gerrit Rietveld, Red and Blue Chair, 1918–1923. The original chair was unlacquered beech wood; only later did it receive its distinctive colors, after Rietveld was already a member of the De Stijl group (1923).

suited in both form and material to industrial manufacturing. Today the Italian firm Cassina is re-issuing the pieces as "design classics."

Architecture

Even before 1917, the architects of De Stijl already ascribed to early modern principles. They admired the work of the American architect Frank Lloyd Wright, pioneer of a new understanding of

J.J.P. Oud, Café de Unie, Rotterdam 1926

spatial organization and of the use of concrete as a structural element in construction. De Stijl architecture derived from the basic form of the cube. Interior organization consists of a series of rooms that open into one another. In both form and function, walls exist not to isolate and limit, but to expand perspectives. For De Stijl, the task of architecture was to integrate space, time, and function; in practice, this tended to result in open-plan rooms.

The Schröder House by Rietveld in Utrecht presents the fullest realization of these ideals. Its design is at once oriented to its interior functions and

Theo van Doesburg and Cornelis van Eesteren, cross-sectional sketch and floor-plan for a house, 1923. The cube form is being dissolved.

Gerrit Rietveld, the Schröder House in Utrecht, 1924. Contrary to De Stijl's theory, the walls are not of concrete, but of traditional brickwork, plastered and painted to create the effect of smooth surfaces.

to the formal principles of De Stijl. The exterior is dominated by large, white rectangular surfaces, horizontally and vertically divided by strong colored lines of railings, window frames, and iron I-beams. The overlapping of the interior rooms is carried to the exterior of the house by projecting flat roofs, balconies, and railings.

The house stands not only as an architectural manifesto of De Stijl principles, but also as a fairly lonely paradigm of modern architecture. Avant-garde ideas never found wide public approval. In design and architecture alike, avant-garde theories were and remain the province of a small intellectual elite. Architects received few contracts on which they didn't have to compromise.

Living room in the upper floor of the Schröder House. While the ground floor consists of separate rooms, the upper floor constitutes an open sequence. The dividing walls are installed on rails and can be moved. The house was supposed to be adaptable to the needs of its inhabitants as well as to the furniture.

Lyonel Feininger, *Cathedrals*, title woodcut for the Bauhaus program, Weimar, 1919. The medieval cathedrals are depicted as a utopian model for a new design.

The Bauhaus (1919–1933)

In Germany, the Bauhaus design became the center of modernism and functionalism. The Bauhaus school laid down principles that still influence industrial design today.

In 1919, Walter Gropius founded the National Bauhaus in Weimar by uniting the Weimar Art Academy and Henry van de Velde's School of Industrial Arts, which had been disbanded in 1915. In the new institution, Gropius wanted to implement his old aim of overcoming historicism through a clear formal language and a new unification of art, handwork, and industry. Toward this end, the Bauhaus developed an entirely new organizational and architectural structure. The basis of Bauhaus education was a preliminary apprenticeship centered on free experimentation with color, form, and material. After the preliminary course, students chose one of the various workshops for carpentry, pottery, metalworking, glasswork, stage design, photography, or commercial art. The goal was to offer an equal education in artistic and handcraft skills. For this reason, each workshop had two directors, an artist who acted as "master of form" and a "master of applied arts." Originally there was no class in architecture. In establishing a balance between art and industry, as well as between aesthetic and social concerns, the various developmental phases of the Bauhaus were marked by regular and recurrent dialectics.

The Bauhaus turned first to Expressionism; like the English arts and crafts movement and the

Karl-Peter Röhl, *The First Insignia of the Bauhaus*, 1919–22. Among the various symbols are also pyramids and a form of swastika.

Schematic representation of the Bauhaus Education Program, 1922.

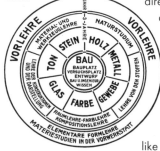

Jugendstil, it initially sought reform in a return to the Middle Ages. In the unification of the arts, architecture was to play the leading role, just as it had in the construction projects of the medieval cathedrals.

The nature of Bauhaus training was determined by the artists whom Gropius first recruited for the Bauhaus: Johannes Itten, Lyonel Feininger, Paul Klee, Georg Muche, and Oskar Schlemmer. Their designs were still strongly oriented toward the applied arts.

Oskar Schlemmer, *Second Signet of the Bauhaus*, used since 1922.

De Stijl at the Bauhaus

An elementary and functional formal language was developed after the beginning of the 1920s, especially through the influence of Theo van Doesburg, who did not actually teach at the Bauhaus, but conducted a De Stijl course in 1922 close to the Bauhaus in Weimar. Van Doesburg radically rejected the artistic direction and subject matter of the Bauhaus training at the time, especially as presented by Itten, and introduced the Bauhaus students to the clear, constructivist forms of the De Stijl movement.

The influence of the Dutch De Stijl movement was broadened after 1922 by the appointment of László Maholy-Nagy to succeed Itten.

Marcel Breuer, chair from wooden slats, 1923. Breuer was an admirer of De Stijl and created numerous chairs in the style of Rietveld between 1921 and 1929.

Walter Gropius (1883–1969), architect and colleague of Peter Behrens. From 1919 to 1928 he was director of the Bauhaus. He designed the new buildings in Dessau in 1925–26, but emigrated in 1934 to London, and in 1937 to the United States where he was an instructor at Harvard University.

1915 – 1933

"The Bauhaus attempts to gather all artistic creation into a single entity—the reunification of all the artistic handwork disciplines—sculpture, painting, the applied arts, and crafts—as indissoluable elements of a new art of building."

Walter Gropius, from the Program of the National Bauhaus in Weimar, 1919

Karl J. Jucker and Wilhelm Wagenfeld, table lamp, 1923–24. The designers' attempt to create an objective form determined by function is evident. Although this lamp was still made by hand, it was constructed from industrially produced materials (metal and glass). Today the lamp is mass-produced.

Marianne Brandt, teapot, 1924. Brass sheet metal with silver-plated interior and an ebony handle. László Moholy-Nagy also introduced atypical combinations of materials into the metal workshop.

The new Bauhaus building in Dessau, designed by Walter Gropius, was an architectonic sensation with a completely glass-faced workshop area facing the street.

Moholy-Nagy was one of the most significant of the constructivists and pursued a rational, technical orientation. Under his leadership, the first industrially useful designs—an indication of the turn toward functionalism—were produced in the metal workshop. Moholy-Nagy discouraged his students from using traditional handicraft materials (wood, silver, clay) in favor of steel tubing, plywood, and industrial glass.

In 1925, under pressure from the new, conservative government, the Bauhaus had to abandon Weimar and it settled in Dessau. In the same year, Marcel Breuer became director of the furniture workshop and designed his first chair made of steel tubing. Breuer was also interested in the possibilities of integrating furniture into the design of built-in kitchens. Accordingly, he shifted the emphasis of Bauhaus education to industrial design and architecture. Next to the promotion of industrial production, his goal was to create economical mass-produced goods for a broad social spectrum. Thus, the Bauhaus at Dessau established its own distribution and sales organization, and a series of products found their way into industrial production. The steel tube chairs were manufactured by Thonet, while Bauhaus wallpaper was produced by the Rasch company.

One of Marcel Breuer's first steel tubing chairs was the famous Wassily Chair, 1925–1926. The seat, back, and side material was at first cloth or steel netting; later leather was used.

László Moholy-Nagy (1895–1946), Hungarian by birth, painter and graphic artist, was director of the Bauhaus metal workshop and instructor of typography, photography, film, and stage design from 1923 to 1928. In addition, he designed all Bauhaus books. In 1928 he left the Bauhaus and opened a graphics studio in Berlin where he created stage designs and exhibit layouts. He also experimented with light, film, and plexiglass, developing the light dimmer switch in 1930. He emigrated to the United States where he founded the New Bauhaus in 1937 and the School of Design in 1938.

Necessity versus luxury

In 1926–27, in spite of growing international recognition, the Bauhaus was suffering under the weight of financial difficulties and internal disagreements about the direction the school should take between art and industry. Furthermore, thus far there was still no architectural program—a shortcoming regretted by many students. In 1927 Gropius established a building department under the direction of Hannes Meyer. Hoping to instill new energy in the face of increasing difficulties, Gropius appointed Meyer director of the entire Bauhaus in 1928. As the new director, Meyer restructured both the organization and the con-

1915 – 1933

Mart Stam, steel tubing chair, S 34, 1926. The copyright of the steel tubing chair without back legs, also known as the "free swinger," has always been a matter of discussion. The idea of such a chair was probably simply in the air at the time, not only at the Bauhaus, because the chair's material and construction seemed to incorporate the philosophy of functionalism.

Hannes Meyer (1899–1954), architect from Basel, worked from 1927 to 1928 as a master of architecture at the Bauhaus before he became director of the Bauhaus itself in 1928. One year later he was forced out of the position because of his political (communist) activities. Afterward, he accepted a professorship at an academy of architecture in Moscow and worked from 1936 to 1939 as an architect in Switzerland, and from 1939 to 1949 as an architect and city planner in Mexico. He is accounted among the most important representatives of functionalistic architecture of the 1920s. His role at the Bauhaus and his contribution to modern architecture are still controversial.

tents of the Bauhaus. He demanded the design of standardized products that could be mass-produced and would satisfy the basic needs of the population. Meyer was a disciple of collective thinking and rejected what he thought of as the artistic-romantic approach. He strove to make Bauhaus instruction more scientific and introduced new subjects such as psychology, sociology, and economics. Under Meyer, thus, in the weaving department, students began to experiment with mixed weaves and synthetic fibers.

Architecture

From architecture Meyer demanded above all the "analysis of social factors." He not only viewed the house as a "machine for living," but looked also at its social aspects. His designs were therefore guided by economic considerations, and he insisted that construction was to use the least expensive materials and to exploit prefabricated building elements. Among his structures are the extension of the worker settlement in Dessau-Törten and the School of the General German Union in Bernau near Berlin (1928–30). Under the pressures of these political and technical aims, art at the Bauhaus was finally pushed into the background. Gropius and Breuer left the Bauhaus in the same year. Gropius, with the help of Josef Albers and Wassily

Walter Gropius, Master House Gropius in Dessau, 1925–26. The architecture developed out of a building-block system based on the cube. The houses of the Bauhaus instructor were generously appointed and relatively expensive to maintain.

Kandinsky, later managed to oust Meyer on political grounds. He was succeeded by Ludwig Mies van der Rohe, who was appointed in 1930. Mies van der Rohe, like Meyer, placed the emphasis entirely on architecture, but did not attach to it the same social and political dimension. In fact, from this point on, students were actually forbidden to engage in political activity. Bauhaus principles and the structure of the education were altered. Mies van der Rohe imposed an authoritative style of leadership.

In spite of this depolitization, many Bauhaus students, in the tradition of Meyer, were members of the Communist Party, and the Bauhaus, along with the entire New Building movement, fell under increasing financial and political pressure. After a temporary move to Berlin, the Bauhaus was finally closed in 1933 under unstoppable pressure from the Nazi regime. Many of the Bauhaus architects emigrated to the United States.

The philosophy of the Bauhaus had in the meanwhile become internationally recognized. The new materials—glass and steel—became, along with the typical simple geometrical shapes of the Bauhaus, important influences on an international modern style. Gropius, Albers, and Mies van der Rohe taught at American universities and in 1937 Moholy-Nagy founded the New Bauhaus in Chicago.

Ludwig Mies van der Rohe (1886–1969), architect, worked in the office of Peter Behrens from 1908 to 1911 and created his first designs for glass high rises in the early 1920s. In 1927 he became the director of the Werkbund exhibit in Stuttgart-Weissenhof, and in 1929 he designed the German pavilion at the World Exhibition in Barcelona. From 1930 to 1933 he was the last director of the Bauhaus in Germany. He then emigrated to the United States. In 1937 he was the director of the Illinois Institute of Architecture in Chicago. Mies van der Rohe was one of the most important architects of the modern style. The leitmotifs of his architecture were transparency and clarity, his motto was "less is more."
Important buildings since World War Two: Lake Shore Drive Apartments, Chicago, 1950–52; Crown Hall, Chicago, 1956; The Seagram Building, New York, 1954–58; The New National Gallery, Berlin, 1962–67.

1915 – 1933

Street in the Worker Settlement at Dessau-Törten, 1926–28.

Architect Margarete Schütte-Lihotzky designed the first German built-in kitchen in 1926 for the city of Frankfurt. Everything was designed to fit into a small apartment. The division of space and the functional and ergonomic design of the furniture and appliances were precisely worked out to ease the job of the housewife by reducing the distances between the fixtures.

The clear, unornamented forms of the modern style had grown out of the theory of functionalism, according to which form arose from function and all decoration was unnecessary—even harmful, because it got in the way of industrial mass production and unnecessarily inflated the cost of manufactured goods. The general assumption was that simple geometric forms were most consistent with the demands of industrial production. The forms and materials of the Bauhaus were justified, especially in a social respect, because modern architecture and industrial mass production were expected to be able to create inexpensive apartments and furniture for the working class. Such an achievement had already been adopted as a goal of earlier reform movements.

Social housing in Germany

The creation of inexpensive living quarters was one of the central goals of avant-garde architecture in Germany between the wars. The city of Frankfurt achieved a comprehensive building

A standard plywood door for the Frankfurt High-Rise Authority, 1925. Ferdinand Kramer relied mostly on plywood, already known from airplane construction, for his standardized furniture and built-in home elements.

program under the direction of Ernst May. The goal was an "apartment for minimum living standards" in which everything would be as inexpensive as possible. For this as well as other apartments, the architect Ferdinand Kramer designed inexpensive and practical household fittings and light fixtures and interchangeable plywood furniture for small rooms in 1925–26. The exhibit, called "The Cheap and Beautiful Apartment," took place in Berlin in 1929. In many larger cities model apartments and housing developments were built to demonstrate to future renters a rational construction with "appropriate and beautiful furniture and fittings."

One of these model developments was the Weissenhof Settlement in Stuttgart, which was built in 1927 as a part of the Werkbund exhibit called "The Apartment." Under the leadership of Mies van der Rohe, the houses were built of industrially prefabricated concrete sections. Among the architects were Jacobus J.P. Oud and Le Corbusier. The exhibit became an international forum of avant-garde architects and designers, and the social housing construction of interwar Germany became a model for American architects.

A new challenge was also the block of flats, or the urban apartment building, with built-in community rooms featuring such amenities as a swimming pool, cafés, and exercise rooms. In 1930 at the Werkbund show in Paris, Gropius exhibited an arrangement of such community

Walter Gropius, a café-bar for a high-rise apartment building at the exhibition of the German Werkbund, Paris, 1930.

1915 – 1933

Walter Gropius, living room of a house in the Weissenhof Settlement, Stuttgart, 1927.

Ludwig Mies van der Rohe,
table of steel tubing with
glass plate, 1927. This table
was presented at the Werkbund Exhibit in Stuttgart.
Shown here is a modern
reproduction by the firm Knoll
International.

1915 – 1933

Ludwig Mies van der Rohe,
Barcelona chair, 1929. This
chair belonged to the German pavilion at the World
Exhibition in Barcelona. It is
made not of steel tubes but of
flat strips of steel welded together by hand, with leather
upholstery. The social aspect
of functionalism took a back
seat to the chair's elegant
appearance.

rooms designed with a lot of glass and steel, light
and air. The presentation of German design
achieved international recognition. With his use
of new materials and cool objective forms,
Gropius addressed a modern metropolitan sense
of life that was developing in the larger cities
around that time—a sense of life that valued the
technical forms of the industrial age as an
aesthetic statement as well.

Functionalism, however, was already
threatening to become yet another kind of
formalism. The new designs were in fact "aes-
theticized" as hallmarks of a new, modern
attitude and as status symbols of the taste of the
intellectual elite.

Ludwig Mies van der Rohe, The German Pavilion at the World
Exhibition in Barcelona, 1929. The architecture demonstrates
Mies van der Rohe's spatial understanding which, like the De
Stijl concept, depends on rooms opening into each other. The
organization works toward the outside. The pavilion included
furniture (also by Mies van der Rohe) whose clarity and cool
material elegance were in perfect harmony with the rational
architecture.

The swift growth in industry and technology had
not only influenced the position of the worker, but
also called forth an entirely new social stratum—
management-level employees with a good income
and a technically oriented, modern, and sporty
attitude—the white-collar worker. The steel tube
chair was exactly suited to this new metropolitan

"In its clear appearance and the beauty of its materials, steel furniture is a living expression of our search for rhythm, appropriateness, hygiene, cleanliness, lightness, simplicity in form. As a material, steel is hard, resistant, durable, and at the same time can follow flexibly the impulses of free design. Well-formed steel furniture possesses an independent aesthetic worth that belongs to itself alone."

Hans Luckhardt, 1931

Ludwig Mies van der Rohe, free-swinging chair, S 533 R, made of steel tubing, with a seat and back of hand-woven reeds, 1927.

class which valued the cool elegance of industrial materials in the expansionary mid-1920s before the financial crash that saw in the end of the decade.

The "international style"

Modern designers, led by Frank Lloyd Wright in the United States and by Adolf Loos and Peter Behrens in Europe, created an international language of form in architecture and design from the 1920s onward. Bauhaus forms became a so-called international style. In 1932, the American architects H.R. Hitchcock and P. Johnson pub-

Marcel Breuer, Alfred and Emil Roth, a living room in a multifamily settlement in Dol-dertal, near Zurich, 1934. The room is bright and open, the furniture light and variable. This arrangement shows how the severe Bauhaus aesthetic of the 1930s took on an increasingly elegant tone.

1915 – 1933

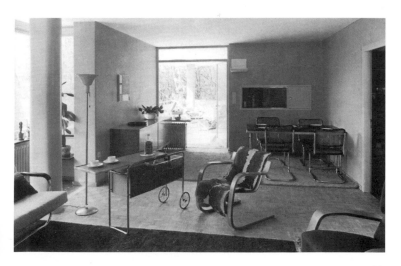

Le Corbusier (pseudonym for Charles Eduoard Jeanneret, 1887–1965) is one of the most important architects of the 20th century and cofounder of so-called purism. Among his important buildings are the Pavillon de l'Esprit Nouveau (1925), and Villa Savoie (1929–31) in Poissy. In the 1950s he turned away from pure geometrical functionalism and toward organic forms, as in the Chapel of Ronchamp, 1950–54.

lished *The International Style*, examining architecture since 1922, while the same two architects organized an exhibition with the same title at the Museum of Modern Art, which was a scant three years old at the time. *The International Style* was initially concerned with architecture: Hitchcock and Johnson insisted that architecture no longer be understood as mass, but as volume. In the future, axial symmetry must give way to a clarity of design that is free of all decoration. Furniture as well was to be free of ornamentation, and to exude clarity, transparency, elegance, and rationality. The ideals were brought to America by Le Corbusier, Mies van der Rohe, Marcel Breuer, and others from France and Germany.

One of the principles of the international style had already been established by Le Corbusier in his book *Vers une architecture*, published in 1922. Le Corbusier favored the high rise and the severe geometrical patterns for façades and layout. His Pavillon de l'Esprit Nouveau at the 1925 Exposition Internationale des Arts Décoratifs in Paris, aroused controversy and indignation. His visionary city planning—for example, the complete rebuilding of Paris—remains controversial among architects and city planners today. Le Corbusier, together with his cousin Pierre Jeanneret and Charlotte Perriand,

Le Corbusier, Pierre Jeanneret and Charlotte Perriand, lounge chair, LC 4, designed 1928. The chrome-plated steel frame supports a recumbent surface with a neck roll covered in black cowhide. A steel base facilitates adjustment. The chair is manufactured today by the Cassina firm.

Le Corbusier, Pierre Jeanneret and Charlotte Perriand, chair, LC3, "Fauteil grand confort, grand modèle," designed 1928, chrome-plated steel tube construction with unattached cushions of black leather. Modern reproduction by the firm Cassina, Milan.

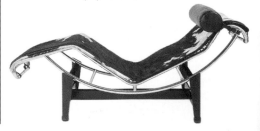

created steel tube furniture pieces that have become modern classics.

In Scandinavia, the more than 200 private and public buildings of the Finnish architect Alvar Aalto established him firmly among the ranks of the architects of the Modern age. He designed his furniture in connection with the building project at hand as an organic component of the architecture. Examples of his interpretations are the stools he designed for the City Library of the former Finnish capital of Lipuri, and the chairs he designed for the Paimio Pulmonary Sanatorium, for which he bent whole plywood surfaces into the form he desired.

Aalto translated the principle and elegance of the free-swinging chair into bent layered birchwood, which, unlike steel tubing, has a warmer glow. Since the mid-1930s his furniture has been manufactured by Artek, a firm Aalto founded.

In the 1930s, however, the leading edge of modern design was found in the United States, in part thanks to the influx of Bauhaus designers forced out of Germany by the Nazi regime. In the following years, the Museum of Modern Art in New York became the trend and taste setter for international design.

Alvar Aalto (1898–1976), one of the most significant architects and designers of the 20th century, defined modern architecture in Finland with his numerous public and private buildings.

1915 – 1933

Alvar Aalto, chair, 406, designed 1935–39: a free-swinging chair of layered wood. The seat and back are of cloth belting.

1921   Coco Chanel introduces Chanel No. 5

1922   Mussolini assumes power in Italy

1923   George Gershwin, *Rhapsody in Blue*

1927   Charles Lindbergh makes the first solo trans-Atlantic flight

1929   World Exhibition in Barcelona

1932   Aldous Huxley, *Brave New World*

1933   Reichstag fire and start of suppression of all opposition in Germany

1936   Outbreak of the Spanish Civil War

1937   Pablo Picasso paints *Guernica* for the Spanish Pavilion at the World Exhibition in Paris

1940   Winston Churchill becomes British prime minister

1941   Japan attacks Pearl Harbor

1944   Beginning of the Allied invasion of Normandy

1945   First electronic digital computer developed in the United States; United States drops atom bombs on Hiroshima and Nagasaki

1925 – 1945

An age of contrasts

In both the United States and Europe, the 1920s and 1930s were decades riddled with contradictions. In Germany, war, revolution, and economic crises resulted in massive unemployment, poverty, and housing shortages. Modern design grew chiefly out of theoretical questions and issues surrounding social reform. In the face of this uneasy milieu, the financial elite maintained its previous life-style, and organized their social lives around culture, entertainment, sport, and a hectic pursuit of pleasure. After Paris, Berlin became the cultural and economic center of Europe.

Left: An age of contrasts: an American working-class family in the Great Depression.

Right: Elegant evening society around a Bugatti motor car, gouache by **Ernst Deutsch Dryden**.

The United States, meanwhile, was full of music and dance: jazz, swing, the Charleston; Benny Goodman, Josephine Baker, and Fred Astaire were as well known in Europe as they were in New York. American popular culture was fast becoming the country's top export. The age of

Otto Arpke, advertising poster for the German airline, Lufthansa, from the 1930s. Travel by airplane was seen as worldly and chic.

Hollywood was dawning with a vengeance; from this California motion picture capital came historical pictures, Busby Berkeley extravaganzas, Marx Brothers comedies, and Astaire and Rogers dance films—all wielding an almost immeasurable influence on life, on fashion, on design, even on morality.

The expansion of international commerce and the development of new transportation systems brought new challenges for design: luxury liners,

The 1920s were absorbed in a taste for the exotic—from exotic woods imported from the tropics to tiger skins and African masks to Josephine Baker and her *Revue Nègre*.

airships and airplanes, luxurious hotel suites, palatial movie theaters, and department stores all had to be planned and outfitted. The global spread of electrification brought an array of products based on new technologies—radios, telephones, televisions, lamps, clocks, appliances—all of which needed to be designed. Now advertisements spread via new media would offer new achievements in fashion, cosmetics, and luxury articles like ciga-

American expatriate dancer Josephine Baker in one of her famous poses that inspired the various small Art Deco sculptures.

Cassandre (A. Mouron), famous Art Deco poster artist, created many posters for travel agencies. Here, the Normandie, considered the most luxurious ocean liner afloat.

1925 – 1945

Edgar Brandt, wrought iron standing lamp with glass bowl by Daum, ca. 1925. Brandt (1880–1960) was an artist and metalsmith; he worked with copper, bronze, and other metals.

rette cases and perfume flasks. This was not only a period of social apartment building, but the age of the great fashion designers, Coco Chanel and Jeanne Lanvin. Design was now applied to modern life itself and, by Italian futurists, to the beauty of speed. Modern design, however, was creating symbols not only for rationality and progress, but also for economic and political power.

Art Deco

In France, where the bourgeois establishment survived the First World War relatively unscarred, a luxurious style of furnishing and decoration reflecting power and a superior life-style emerged. The French skilled craftsmen were also seeking to confront international competition on the world market. Thus, at the behest of the great Parisian stores, the conservative Compagnie des Art Français together with the leading design artists of the time decided to stage an exhibition—in part in reaction to the establishment of the German Werkbund in the same year. The Exposition des Arts Décoratifs et Industriels Modernes (from which the luxurious style of the 1960s derived its name retrospectively) had to be postponed for several reasons, not least of which was the war. But finally in 1925, amid much ado, the exposition opened in Paris.

Exponents of modernism were not well served here: the Bauhaus was not even represented, the

For his pavilion at the Exposition Internationale des Arts Décoratifs, built by architect Pierre Patout, Jacques-Emile Ruhlmann designed costly accoutrements for the "Apartment of a Rich Art Collector."

United States showed no interest, and the modern Pavillon de l'Esprit Nouveau by Le Corbusier was critically interpreted as provocation and exiled to the periphery of the exhibition.

Extravagantly crafted art handworks

Art Deco was diammetrically opposed to the goals of modernism. Far from striving for the mass industrial production of wares, the movement focused on exclusive, artfully designed, individually crafted wares, made of expensive and precious materials like snakeskin, ivory, bronze, crystal, and exotic woods. Eventually some Art Deco pieces came to incorporate modern materials such as steel, glass, and plastics in extravagant combinations, but the aim at all times was to exploit their decorative value, and at no time to explore their more functional utility.

Ornamentation and decoration

In its choice of forms, Art Deco at first drew its models from various historical epochs and exotic cultures—not unlike the recent Postmodern movement. Although Art Deco certainly drew freely from art nouveau, under the influence of cubism, constructivism, and futurism, art nouveau's characteristic curved lines gave way to abstract geo-

Louis Süe and André Mare, table clock of gilded bronze on an onyx stand, ca. 1925.

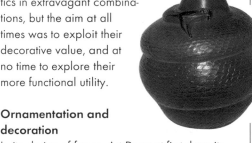

René Lalique (1860–1945), colored glass vase, ca. 1925. Even in the period when art nouveau was still popular, Lalique was one of the best-known glass artists. After the First World War he set up a factory in Alsace where he developed complex techniques for glass cutting, coloring, and etching.

1925 – 1945

Jacques-Emile Ruhlmann (1901–84), desk of Macasser wood and fire-brazed bronze, ca. 1926.

René Lalique, perfume bottle, Firebird. Lalique, like other Art Deco artists, was inspired by Stravinsky's ballet, performed in Paris by the Ballets Russes.

metrical stylization, expressive zig-zag lines, and dynamic streamlining. The new favorite forms were geometric ornaments based on hexagons, octagons, ovals and circles, triangles and rhombuses. But Art Deco also borrowed freely from classicism, pre-Columbian and Egyptian cultures, and African art, and thus developed in diverse directions: the classical-elegant, the exotic-expressive, and increasingly, the modern.

It is not surprising, thus, that art historians have had a hard time agreeing about where Art Deco fits in chronologically. Some date the beginning of the style to 1910; others say it did not coalesce until after 1918. There is little argument, however, that it peaked in the 1920s and 1930s—although certainly, in the course of time, what began as an

Jean Prouvé, adjustable chair, Fauteil de Grand Repos, ca. 1930 (modern reproduction by Tecta). Prouvé (1901–84) was a metal-working artist and saw furniture as machinery. He preferred steel tubing and sheeting as materials and, like Le Corbusier and Eileen Gray, was an exponent of modernism, but is often also considered a representative of Art Deco.

extravagant style increasingly adopted more modern elements, employed more industrial materials, and worked its way into popular taste.

All that glitters

Now arose a seemingly uncountable number of designers and craftsmen, none of whom are very easily categorized. The best-known and most expensive furniture designer was the traditionalist Jacques-Emile Ruhlmann who, along with René Lalique and Edgar Brandt, dominated at the 1925 Exposition Internationale des Arts Déco-

Pierre Chareau, chair from palisander and nut wood with red leather uphostery, ca. 1928.

ratifs in Paris, with Louis Süe and André Mare, both of whom pursued an extremely sumptuous style, also drawing a fair amount of attention.

While most of the designers who garnered acclaim at the 1925 Exposition were basically traditionalist designers, there was also a group of Art Deco exponents whose more modernist approach cast them in the role of outsiders, including Pierre Chareau, Eileen Gray, and Jean Prouvé.

High fashion

With growing numbers of self-possessed, self-confident working women, movie stars, and women married to rich and nouveau riche industrialists and war profiteers, fashion as an area of design grew as well. The great couturiers, such as Poiret, Chanel, Lanvin, and Schiaparelli, number among the influential personalities of Art Deco.

Art Deco international

Art Deco was originally a French phenomenon. Its forms, however, found great resonance elsewhere in Europe and in the United States in the early decades of the 20th century. One of the most famous examples of the spreading of Art Deco is in fact well beyond the normal scope of Western influence—the Palace of the Maharaja of Indore. This Indian prince had studied at Oxford, where he had become acquainted with the young German architect Eckart Muthesius. The prince commissioned Muthesius to build and complete the interior design of his palace. Muthesius enlisted the assistance of some of the best-

Eileen Gray (1879–1976), an Irish architect and designer, after studying in London, moved to Paris where she became one of the most important designers and theoreticians of modernism. She worked together with J.J.P. Oud and Le Corbusier and designed the first furniture of steel tubing as early as 1925, long before any of her colleagues had adopted this medium. In 1972 she was named "Royal Designer to Industry" by the Royal Society of Art in London. In 1987 the Museum of Modern Art in New York accepted her Adjustable Table E 1027 into its design collection.

1925 – 1945

Adjustable Table E 1027, chrome-plated steel tube structure with a glass top (modern reproduction by Classicon, Munich).

Eckart Muthesius, library chair for the Palace of Indore, ca. 1930 (modern reproduction by Classicon, Munich).

Eckart Muthesius, floor lamp for the Palace of Indore.

known French designers, and himself designed an extravagant line of furniture, including a seating group with red lacquer and black plastic, several lamps, wall coverings, and library chairs with built-in reading lamps and ashtrays.

Industrial mass production

In England, Germany, and Italy, Art Deco design was esteemed as an expression of modern elegance, and in the course of time, the manufacture of popular mass wares from new materials such as aluminum and Bakelite became increasingly popular. Before long, the market offered fashion jewelry, cigarette cases, radio housings, and perfume bottles with classic-geometrical shapes and expressionistic zigzag patterns or ornamental synthetic inlays imitating ivory or tortoiseshell.

Art Deco in the United States

The ideas of European modernism were an issue for only a few avant-garde American architects who had been carefully observing the Bauhaus movement and other trends in the 1920s. Although Frank Lloyd Wright was certainly in the vanguard of modern architecture, and although steel-framed skyscrapers were being erected in American cities at the turn of the century, the vast major-

1925 – 1945

Coffee machine Mocha Express, by Alfonso and Renato Bialetti, aluminum and black plastic, ca. 1930. Originally finished by hand, the model went into mass production after 1945 and retains the same eight-sided Art Deco form today. It is the most common of all Italian household objects.

ity of buildings continued to be decorated with historistical window ledges, bays, alcoves, and Gothic arches until the end of the decade. New York's ostentatious neo-Gothic Woolworth Building (1913) is an example of the still prevailing taste in American architecture.

Furniture and objects for interior design were still designed primarily to suit the taste of the middle and upper classes, who persisted in preferring the fine handwork of the colonial style or a historical European style. Aside from the vestiges of the arts and crafts movement, the American skilled crafts experienced no strong push toward reform. The philosophy of modernism spread only with the influx of Bauhaus designers fleeing Hitler's Germany. But modernism did spread in the United States, and once it spread, it took hold. In 1932, the Cranbrook Academy was founded near Detroit, under the direction of Finnish architect Eliel Saarinen. And Saarinen saw the academy as an outpost of the Bauhaus. Saarinen's Bauhaus' industrial, functional influence is visible today in many of his American works, including the circular chapel and concrete dome at the Massachusetts

A typical 1930s radio cabinet made of Bakelite.

Perfume bottle for the gentleman (Northwoods Company, Chicago), ca. 1927. The "cubist" head was made of Bakelite, the bottle of brown glass.

1925 – 1945

A page from the catalog of the English housewares company, Bandalasta, which advertised the inexpensive prices and durability of its products.

Bakelite: One of the first purely synthetic substances, Bakelite was invented in 1907 by Leo Baekeland. In the 1920s and 1930s, the chemical industry developed other synthetic resins such as phenol resin and vitrolite, which also became very popular. These new materials proved ideal for everyday objects. Malleable, durable, and inexpensive, the new plastics were wellsuited to inexpensive reproduction of Art Deco style.

Lee Lawrie, relief over the entrance of Rockefeller Center in midtown Manhattan. In contrast to the building's modern objective exterior, the interior is replete with elaborate decoration. Sculptures and reliefs in Art Deco style adorn the entrances, halls, and the basement atrium.

1925 – 1945

The Chrysler Building in New York has a richly decorated exterior. The building was designed to reflect the elegance of the Chrysler automobile and the economic strength of the company.

Institute of Technology, the TWA terminal at New York's Kennedy Airport, and IBM's Thomas J. Watson Research Center in a suburb of New York City.

The richly ornamented Art Deco style was more readily adopted than was modern functionalism, at least in architecture and interior design. Since the end of the 1920s, the "great" architectural firms were building ostentatious buildings in the style of Art Deco in New York and Miami, including huge skyscrapers and

New York's Great Art Deco Buildings
- Radio City Music Hall, 1931. Architect: Raymond Hood
- Empire State Building, 1932. Architects: Shreve, Lamb & Harmon
- Rockefeller Center, 1931. Architect: Raymond Hood
- Chrysler Building, 1930. Architect: William Van Alen

splendid movie palaces. The closest model for this kind of architecture is probably found in the style of the large luxury liners, with their bows and railings. The buildings, like the ocean liners, used noble woods and marble, often with brass inlays, colorful glass and colored tiles, as well as geometrical Expressionistic forms.

In the 1930s, the rich, decorative art nouveau style evolved into a more sober American style. In response to the worldwide economic crisis, more objective and less expensive methods of construction followed in the train of governmental measures. Similarly, as a result of economic and political considerations, a combination of Art Deco forms and the new streamlined form found its way into many mass-produced products: in fact, an American Art Deco basically entails streamlining.

Modern industrial design

In the United States, modern design pursued its own course. Though industrial designers may have been affected by European influences, here more than anywhere else design was driven by consumer behavior, through technical advances, and—more than is sometimes realized—through the subtle and not so subtle Hollywood influence on the aesthetic sensibility of whole generations.

Jacques Delamare, a radiator cover in the Chanin Building, New York, 1927. The terraced ornamentation reflects the architectonics of the exterior.

S. L. Rothafels and Donald Deskey, a suite in Radio City Music Hall, ca. 1932. At Radio City, the elegance and luxury of Art Deco mix with the objective aesthetic of functionalism.

Design and technology

While the First World War had seriously impaired technical and economic development in Europe, the United States in the early 1920s stood far above other industrial nations in the level of its technology. In the 1930s, most middle-class households owned electric equipment, including radios, refrigerators, toasters, and washing machines. The boundary between furniture design and industrial design dissolved early here. Mass production with new inexpensive materials for mass needs was a foregone conclusion—not a topic of debate—and toward the end of the

An elevator door in the Chrysler Building. The inlay work uses stylized Egyptian motifs like palms and lotus blossoms.

Norman Bel Geddes, bus (1931) and passenger automobile (1934) in streamlined water-drop form. Such models were exhibited at the 1939 World's Fair in New York.

1920s a burgeoning advertising industry already supported itself on the findings of market research. In addition to advertising and packaging, the stylistic design of products acquired ever greater importance to satisfy the demands of the moneyed classes.

It was not long ago that the design of automobiles and other consumer products was pragmatically oriented around their function and the technical requirements of the assembly line. Witness the ever-practical, ever-functional Model T Ford, a no-frills model that faced no real competition back in 1913. In the

Walter Dorwin Teague, a radio receiver made of wood, metal, and blue glass, 1936.

1925 – 1945

> "Of two products that are the same in price, function and quality, whichever is more beautiful will sell better."
>
> *Raymond Loewy, 1929*

1920s and 1930s, however, design became increasingly critical as a factor to distinguish among the expanding competition. Whereas in Europe, design reforms and the public debate surrounding them had always been subsumed in discussions of social aspects and function, in the United States design was first and foremost a marketing factor. A new understanding of design developed through the pressure of the economic crisis of 1929.

Raymond Loewy, locomotive, S 1, Pennsylvania Railroad Company, 1938.

The Great Depression

After the Wall Street crash of 1929 and the resulting Great Depression, the federal government wanted to crank up consumption to stimulate the economy. It became almost patriotic to design consumer commodities in such a way that their market presentation would motivate customers to buy. We call this reworking and redesigning of the product "styling," and the optimal form of styling adopted by American designers in this period was the streamline. In fact, streamlining was the invention of the Italian futurists, but American industry was able to tool up for mass production of streamlined designs thanks to its superior resources and technology.

Raymond Loewy, pencil sharpener, 1933.

The streamlined form

As a sign of progress and dynamism, streamlining was applied to a vast array of products, from buses to baby carriages, from coffee machines to pencil sharpeners, and was employed by architects. New materials such as plywood, plastics, and sheet metal supported the use of streamlining, and became the medium through which American industrial designers created a new direction that had little to do with the function of the object, but was primarily intended to instill (even subliminally) a belief in progress and trust in the

1925 – 1945

Raymond Loewy, milk centrifuge for the International Harvester Company, 1939.

Streamlined form: The idealized water-drop form was able to minimize wind resistance. Streamlining is the result of aerodynamic research in airplane and automobile manufacturing since the First World War. Since the 1930s, streamlining has been used in the "styling" of various products to symbolize a dynamic faith in the future; in the 1950s it was being used by all the industrialized nations.

Styling: In design, this term means the formal reworking of a product under purely aesthetic and market-oriented considerations in order to make it more attractive to the consumer. The term appeared in the United States after the Great Depression when industry wanted to boost sales. Because it promoted consumption, functionalists were strongly opposed to the concept.

Henry Dreyfuss (1903–72) was one of the few designers who did not come from the advertising industry. Dreyfuss was a theatrical designer and opened his design office in New York in 1929. Since the 1940s he focused on the theory of ergonomics. In 1957 he published *The Measure of Man*.

Norman Bel Geddes (1893–1958) was a painter, advertising artist, and stage designer. He created the most significant of the streamlined automobile and train models. In 1939 he designed the Futurama Building of General Motors at the New York World's Fair.

Norman Bel Geddes and Albert Kahny, the General Motors Pavilion at the 1939 New York World's Fair.

U.S. economy in order to steer the country out of the depression. This became one of the pillars of "the American way of life."

This optimism reached a peak in 1939 at the New York World's Fair, which was called "Building the World of Tomorrow." Between 1920 and 1940, American industrial design developed along a swift path that essentially disentangled it from the theories of European design. Through the 1950s, streamlining remained the emblem of this attitude toward progress.

Most of the leading American industrial designers of the time came from the field of advertising. Walter Dorwin Teague, for example, had worked for over 20 years doing commercial drafting before he secured his first design contract with Kodak. Before the Second World War, he and Raymond Loewy were the most prominent industrial designers in the United States. Teague created the Ford Pavilion at the 1939 New York World's Fair, as well as cameras for Kodak, gas stations for Texaco, and the Boeing 707 airplane, among other works.

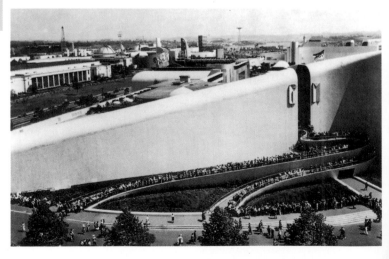

Design in the Third Reich

While design in the United States strove under marketing pressure to "beautify" and modernize an array of technically sophisticated products in order to sell more of them, the German National Socialists consciously exploited the ideological dimensions of design for political purposes. Laws ridding state offices of non-Aryan artists or establishing new institutions like the "Beauty of Work Office" or the "National Homestead Authority" served in the creation of a new *Volkskultur* ("folk culture").

Design under the Third Reich was characterized by what at first glance appear to be paradoxes but which, on closer scrutiny, all served an important function in the Nazi ideology. It is not possible, however, to speak of an inherent Nazi style, because historicist and modern forms were utilized and even combined depending on the purpose at hand.

The days of modern architecture in social housing projects came to an abrupt end, replaced by small single houses with gable roofs according to the "Blood and Soil" ideology.

In the showy architecture of Hitler's massive public buildings, a monumental pseudo-classicism dominated. In the domestic sphere, a mixture of home-baked rusticity and plain objectivism corresponding to the petty bourgeois notion of homeliness was just as useful as Nazi economic and defense policies in preparing for the war. Furniture was made of wood or plywood because steel was used only for arms production after 1935–36.

The Nazi stance toward the modern

The Nazis closed the Bauhaus on political grounds, and the expon-

Arno Breker, *Comrades*, relief, 1940. A shallow, monumental pseudo-classicism was supposed to convey Nazi values.

1925 – 1945

Albert Speer, German Pavilion, Paris World's Fair, 1937.

Summer uniform of a foreman of the Hitler Youth. The organization and imposition of uniform dress on all areas of life characterized the Nazis' system of "governing."

A model apartment in Dorf im Warndt, Saarland, Germany, 1936. A mixture of objectivism and homeland-rusticity dominated private life.

1925 – 1945

ents of functionalism as well as the avant-garde were forced to emigrate. But while it rejected modern art, the Nazi regime readily adopted the striving of functionalism toward simplicity and clarity, toward standardization through cheap materials and mass production. For simplicity and plainness, the feeling of usefulness was as consistent with the ideology of the Nazi *Volkskultur* as with the requirements of industrial production. Hitler was able to adopt many of the goals of the reform movements since many of the reformers' positions were already closely aligned with the nationalist-conservative philosophy. Many members of the German Werkbund had organized themselves before 1933 into a "Union for the Struggle for German Culture," while others hoped to preserve a niche for themselves through their voluntary political conformity or later turned up in the "Beauty of Work" department.

The "Beauty of Work" department

Large businesses owned by non-Jewish families were left in their owners' possession, just as the

economic and property structures were left largely untouched; of course, businesses owned by Jewish families, it need hardly be pointed out, suffered quite a different fate—beyond the scope of our discussion of design. Instead, the Nazis demanded a greater concentration of large firms because the goal of the economic policy was to increase production in all areas. It was the job of the "Beauty of Work" department to use advertising campaigns and guideline booklets to govern the standardization and modernization of the factories. And in spite of the Blood and Soil ideology, suitable functionalist forms along with the new materials and production techniques were employed for industrial mass production. To prove the government's social agenda, the office also conducted campaigns for improvement of working conditions.

The Volkswagen

The Volkswagen was supposed to be a bold "stroke of National Socialism," a promise to the people after years of deprivation that soon everyone could own an automobile. Ferdinand Porsche had worked on the idea of an inexpensive car for the mass of the population, something that would be similar to the Ford Model T since the 1920s. The auto was to be streamlined and easy to assemble. Porsche's prototypes, however, were rejected by the great automobile companies because they did not think the car would be profitable, or (like Opel) because they were working on a similar product themselves, so Porsche turned to the government. After a long period of hesitation,

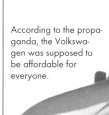

According to the propaganda, the Volkswagen was supposed to be affordable for everyone.

Christian Dell, desk lamp, 1930. In spite of their origin in the Third Reich, many of the objective functionalistic forms of the 1920s and 1930s would draw little notice if produced today.
Right: electric fan, 1938.

1925 – 1945

Hitler, who had decided upon full motorization and autobahn construction as a propagandistic measure to generate jobs and as a strategic preparation for war, supported the project. The streamlined shape of the car was accepted by the Nazis and dubbed "bioform," which was supposed to suggest both the racial and the technical superiority of Germany.

In order to produce what was in reality an unprofitable car, the Volkswagen factory, founded in 1938, was supported by the state. After 1939, the Reich launched a program allowing people to contribute five marks a week toward the price of the car. However, the approximately one third of a million "Volkswagen savers" never did become the proud owners of their own car: the money instead was channeled into the production of Jeeps—needed by the military. So much for a car for every family!

An advertisement for the Volkswagen, 1937, known to most of the world as the "Beetle."

A radio for the people

The *Volksempfänger*, literally "People's Radio," was also a modern industrial product: Walter Maria Kersting had developed it in 1928. The radio's functionalistic, clearly organized casing was made out of the modern synthetic resin Bakelite, while the rounded corners and curved lines of the dial area reveal an Art Deco influence. The apparatus was conceived for mass consumption in terms of technology and price. It differed from comparable American and French radios in that it was designed to receive only local stations. The "People's Radio," in other words, had only one purpose: it was, according to Joachim Petsch, the "most important instrument for fascist media policy." The radio was to provide "fellow citizens" with information disseminated by the radio companies. These, of course, were all under the control of the Ministry for Public Enlightenment and Propaganda. To put a radio (and thus a propagandistic mouthpiece) in every home, the government subsidized its production and offered a time payment plan.

The products of the Nazi period—furniture, technical equipment, and industrial products—were not produced in state factories and thus evince no single style. Their character depended on their function in the perfect machine of a system that could produce at will both highly modern technical weapons and extermination facilities, decked over with a spurious pseudo-biological, pseudo-classicist, and pseudo-mystical ideology. It is not the form of the objects, but their political function, that converted the architecture, industrial products, and items of daily life and the Aryan image at the root of the Nazis' racial insanity into a "Nazi style."

Walter Maria Kersting, People's Radio, 1928. The cabinet was made of Bakelite with Art Deco overtones.

1925 – 1945

"All Germany Listens to the Führer." An advertising poster for the "People's Radio." Even in commercial design the Nazis utilized modern methods; here the montage technique of John Heartfield is adapted to Nazi propaganda purposes.

1945   End of the Second World War

1946   Nuremberg trials

1947   The Marshall Plan begins to help rebuild Europe

1949   Mao Tse-tung proclaims the People's Republic of China

1950   Start of the Korean War

1951   First color televisions sold in the United States

1952   Ernest Hemingway, *The Old Man and the Sea*

1953   Workers' uprising in East Berlin; East Germany is overrun by Soviet tanks

1954   Federico Fellini, *La Strada*; the United States builds the first nuclear submarine *Nautilus*

1955   *Rebel Without a Cause* actor James Dean dies in a car crash

1956   Soviet troops suppress the uprising in Hungary

1957   The Treaty of Rome establishes the European Economic Union

1945 – 1960

Aerial photograph of Hiroshima, 1947, two years after the dropping of the atom bomb.

The 1950s

The postwar period and the 1950s, nostalgically misnamed the "Swinging Fifties," brought about deep changes not only in politics but also in international style. In the early part of this era, the primary concern of the defeated Axis nations, Germany, Italy, and Japan, was recovery; they had to concentrate on basic needs: food, shelter, and rebuilding their economy, their nation, and their government. Many of their factories had been destroyed or dismantled, and raw materials as well as workers were in short supply.

In Germany, the designer utopias of the 1920s and 1930s had been nipped in the bud by the Third Reich, as well as in the occupied countries of France and Holland; in the

The ruins of Dresden, 1945.

Soviet Union, social utopia fast melted in the face of Stalinism.

The United States, on the other hand, survived the war comparatively unharmed, despite human casualties. It was the one victor whose mainland and economy were intact, and this allowed it to assume the role of economic leader and to establish its economic and political hegemony well into the 1950s. In the design arena, important representatives of the Bauhaus had already immigrated to the United States during the Nazi years, and it was here that they pursued the international style in modernist architecture and design.

For this reason, after the war, an emigrant modernism was exported back to Europe from the United States, simultaneously spreading the American approach to design as a factor in marketing and sales. The so-called American way of life influenced almost all areas of life and culture, especially in Germany and Italy: music and art, patterns of consumption, and daily living. The influence of the American motion picture and advertising industries on ideals of beauty and waves of fashion in Europe and elsewhere can hardly be overstated. Coca-Cola and Lucky Strike became symbols of a new international life-style.

New York, 1949. In contrast to Europe and Japan, the United States homeland did not suffer physical destruction and subsequent shortages of food and shelter.

In the Europe of 1949, such richly supplied food stores were nowhere to be found.

1945 – 1960

The American air bridge for the supply of West Berlin during the Berlin blockade of 1948–49.

Harry Bertoia, chair 421, made from steel chrome netting, with pillows. Bertoia's designs pursued a sense of lightness in space.

Eero Saarinen's one-legged, organically shaped Tulip Chairs (1956) with polyester seats were supposed to bring order to the area under the seat.

Charles and Ray Eames, La Chaise, 1948. Prototype of hard rubber covered with synthetic covering. The similarity to the sculptures of Henry Moore is unmistakeable.

1945 – 1960

Charles Eames (1907–78), architect and designer, with his layering of wood and finishes made of synthetic materials, is one of the best-known furniture designers of the 20th century. From 1924 to 1926 he studied at Washington University in St. Louis, and since 1936 at the Cranbrook Academy of Arts in Bloomfield Hills, Michigan. In 1941 he married Ray Kaiser, with whom he designed a number of chairs, children's toys and advertising posters. They are also quite well known for their short experimental film, *Powers of Ten* (1968). Eames had collaborated since 1946 with the furniture manufacturer, Herman Miller, for whom he designed pieces out of chrome steel tubing as well as bent plywood (e.g., "Plywood Group") and polyester ("Lounge Chair," 1956, and "Aluminum Group," 1958).

Organic design in home furnishings

By the 1930s, with Hitler's unrelenting choke hold on his own nation and much of Europe, and the flight of modernism out of Germany, the United States assumed world leadership in art, architecture, and design. The New World, however, was much less inclined to frame the attendant social questions of modern design in extreme or dogmatic terms.

New York's Museum of Modern Art, founded in 1929, moved into its own building in 1939. Henceforth, MOMA determined what was avant-garde. Since 1934, the museum possessed a comprehensive design collection and in 1940 it organized a design competition with the support of New York's exclusive department store, Bloomingdale's. Under the title "Organic Design in Home Furnishings," the competition sought new contemporary forms of home furnishings, up-

holstery, and related items. The judges of the contest, as it turned out, showed little interest in the severe geometrical forms of functionalism, but in flowing light lines that bore some relation to the human body. The prize was awarded to Eero Saarinen and Charles Eames for their organically curved wooden shell chair, which united beauty with comfort. Both Saarinen and Eames came from the Cranbrook Academy near Detroit and, along with Harry Bertoia, were among the outstanding exponents of the new organic style. They worked with materials like polyester, aluminum, and plywood. Their furniture was first produced after 1945 as the war shortages came to an end, and new techniques of working with wood and synthetic materials, developed by Eames for the navy, enabled the manufacture of soft, curved forms. Firms such as Herman Miller and Knoll International supported the work of the Cranbrook Academy and mass-produced many designs. Miller and Knoll became the most important manufacturers of modern furniture.

The forms of modern art, meanwhile, also found their way into architecture, advertising, and design. Models were directly adapted from contemporary artists such as Henry Moore and Alexander Calder, or they came in indirectly through show window arrangements of stores such as Bloomingdale's or Bonwit Teller.

Charles Eames, lounge chair, with seat of palisander wood, and leather upholstery, 1956. Eames designed the chair, symbol of comfort, for his friend, movie director Billy Wilder. Modern reproduction by the firm Vitra, Weil am Rhine, Switzerland.

Organic-dynamic forms also in architecture: the interior of Frank Lloyd Wright's Guggenheim Museum in New York City, 1956–59.

1945 – 1960

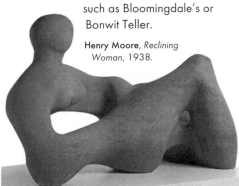

Henry Moore, *Reclining Woman*, 1938.

"With chairs, one's task is to solve chiefly functional problems …, but if one looks closely, they are also studies in space, form and metal."

Harry Bertoia

A 1957 Cadillac with tailfins and rocket-shaped rear lights—the quintessence of the American dream car.

The American way of life

By the 1930s, the United States had developed its own understanding of design which, in contrast to European approaches, focused on styling as a means of increasing profits. The goal was design for mass consumption. Although many representatives of European modernism were active in exile here, and the international style was further developed here, the prewar American aesthetic ideals in industrial design—streamlined and new organic forms—were still preferred. The great names of the 1930s—Teague, Dreyfuss, Bel Geddes, and Loewy—continued to dictate the rules of American design.

Although the United States had suffered far less physical and material damage than Europe

Portable television by General Electric, ca. 1955. The 1950s trend toward miniaturization started in the United States and was perfected by Japanese industry.

1945 – 1960

"Just what is it that makes today's home so different, so appealing?" 1956. English artist Richard Hamilton became the father of pop art with this early collage, offering a critical and ironical commentary on the world of conspicuous consumption.

and Japan during World War II, the country nonetheless struggled in the transition from a wartime to a peacetime economy. Many firms that had been completely tooled for the war effort, and had been forbidden to carry on civil research, were hardly able to survive the transition to the peacetime technologies.

Consumption and progress

The shortages caused by the war provided for a postwar wave of consumption, but by the early 1950s the most important needs had been satisfied and industry found itself having to constantly revive consumer demand through new models, forms, and technical improvements. With the blessing of the marketing and advertising sectors, planned obsolescence was designed into American consumer goods. To foster continual sales and sustain the seemingly burgeoning economy, the role of advertising increased, and with it the role of package design.

The most important industry sectors were automobiles and the ever trusty American home. The dream car, with an airplane nose and imposing tailfins, appeared on the market, while the dream home was overrun by electrical appliances that were supposed to make the housewife's life easier. The rapid development of television and transistor technology also promised continually growing markets—until the Japanese manufacturers began to move into these fields as early as the 1950s and competed with the American electronic industry with ever smaller equipment. Through the end of the 1950s, however, the signs still pointed to prosperity and the American economy looked optimistically forward to the future.

The "ideal" middle-class American living room of the 1950s, a housewife with a vacuum cleaner. In the lower right corner, barely visible, is an organically shaped coffee table by Isamu Noguchi (1949), manufactured by Herman Miller.

"Styling as Incentive to Buy." The happy housewife finds electrical appliances by Westinghouse under the Christmas tree.

1945 – 1960

The evolution of the Shell Oil Company logos (Loewy's design is at right; © Shell International Petroleum Company, London)

Born in Paris, Raymond Loewy became the quintessential American designer. His ideas helped form the image of an "American way of life" and made Loewy one of the most successful designers of the 20th century.

Loewy had a lifelong fascination with modern technology and, unlike European reformers, wanted to "reconcile" the consumer with technology through a pleasant product exterior—that is, through styling. He was also the first designer to base his work on modern market analysis and introduced his products to the market by way of large-scale advertising campaigns. He reworked many products, giving them a new, attractive exterior to make them more "beautiful" and thereby to increase sales and, of course, profits; his motto was "Never leave well enough alone." For Loewy, beauty was simplicity—but

The Lucky Strike cigarette package, 1942.

not dryness. In this he differed considerably from the concept of, for example, the Academy for Design in Ulm.

From Paris to New York
Loewy left Paris in 1919 for the United States, where he first worked as a shop window designer for Macy's Department Store and as a

> "The most reliable appliance has simplicity and quality, does what is demanded of it, is economical to use, easy to maintain, and just as easy to repair. ... It also sells best and looks good."
>
> *Raymond Loewy, 1951*

fashion draftsman for *Harper's Bazaar*.

Raymond Loewy Associates
In 1929 Loewy became art director of the Westinghouse Electric Company in New York, and in the same year founded his own firm, Raymond Loewy Associates. His first commission was to rework a copy machine for the firm of Gestetner. Contracts for numerous other firms followed: designs for a wide range of commodities from refrigerators to automobiles to locomotives, gas stations,

and overall corporate images. In the 1930s Loewy was an outstanding representative of the streamlined form and developed the concept of "styling." He also used the advertising media to improve his own image. He was often criticized by more severe functionalists for this image making, as well as for his use of "styling."

The American Dream

After the Second World War Loewy finally emerged as the United States' number one industrial designer. With his Coca-Cola soda dispenser (1947), Greyhound bus (1950), and his packaging and advertisement for Lucky Strike, he created the icons of the American dream. His book *Never Leave Well Enough Alone* appeared in 1951, permanently securing his stature and success.

Raymond Loewy in an ad in *Time* magazine.

Coca Cola soda fountain dispenser designed for the firm of Dole de Luxe, 1947: the dispenser is dynamic, like an outboard motor.

There's no business like big business

In the 1960s and 1970s, as consumers became more critical, Loewy remained true to his motto. He continually corrected innumerable package designs and company logos. In addition to commissions from the oil companies, British Petroleum, Exxon, and Shell, he was contracted for advisory work; for example, for NASA he developed concepts for the space shuttle and for Skylab. He also taught at various universities and academies. In 1974 he designed the Russian automobile Moskwitch, thus becoming the first designer from the West to receive a Soviet contract.

Loewy's Best-Known Designs

Gestetner copier; S1 locomotive of the Pennsylvania Railroad; Lucky Strike cigarette package; Coca Cola soda fountain dispenser; Shell Oil Company logo; Studebaker Avanti; Greyhound bus; Canada Dry soda bottle; Spar logo.

The Greyhound Scenicruiser, 1954.

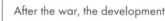

The Italian economic miracle

After the war, the development of design in Italy, which had contributed little to the history of design before World War II, was stormy. Still, after a turbulent decade, this country emerged as one of the foremost design nations. The Italian drive was to be modern, at any price—a tendency whose roots reached back to the futurist movement.

Unlike in Germany, industrialization began very late in Italy, and the transition from handcraft to industrial production was not effected in many sectors until after the war. Italy was also hindered by a problematic north–south schism. Industrially advanced cities like Milan or Turin were all located in the rich north, which, in the first ten to fifteen years after the war, experienced an economic expansion centered on two crucial industrial arenas—export and design. The flexibility of the Italian worker and industrial structure, coupled with low wages and American aid, enabled Italy to something altogether new.

The influence of the United States was not confined to a purely economic role. In fact, the out-

A 1955 Vespa, 125 ccm. The first model was designed in 1946 by Corradino D'Ascanio for the firm Piaggio.

1945 – 1960

Hollywood enthusiastically adopted the "Italian style." Right, a scene from *Roman Holiday* (1953) with Audrey Hepburn and Gregory Peck on a Vespa.

pourings of the motion picture industry, with Hollywood's steady outpouring of images and ideals, had an enduring effect on the Italian feel for life. American patterns of consumption were transformed by Italian characteristics into an independent and finally unparalleled success in design. By 1955, the "Italian line" had become the international expression of a cultivated and cosmopolitan life-style.

The first Italian industry to experience growth was steel, and with it, the production of technical commodities such as cars, typewriters, and motorcycles. Perhaps the best-known Italian postwar products were the Vespa Scooter and the Fiat 500. Soon furniture and fashion also became Italian export hits. Throughout the United States and Europe people wanted Italian suits and dresses, drove Vespas or Lambrettas, and drank espresso. The Italian auto builder Pininfarina had studied in the United States and subsequently set new international standards for sports cars with the softly molded but powerful forms of the Alfa Romeo, the Lancia, and the Ferrari.

Gió Ponti, prototype of a coffee machine for the Pavoni firm, 1947. This gleaming chrome organic-dynamic "sculpture" of a coffee machine became a trademark of the espresso bars of the 1950s.

Marcello Nizzoli's typewriter, Lettera 22, for Olivetti was distinguished with the Compasso d'Oro in 1954.

1945 – 1960

Art and design

Where American design tended to be market-oriented, and German design tended to be theoretical, the Italian style was marked by improvisation and by a cultural tradition that had never been accustomed to strictly separating art, design, and economics—beauty and function. Furthermore, there was no specific design education in Italy; the majority of the designers were architects.

In the fashion industry in particular, the combination of artistic creativity and the tradition of

Marcello Nizzoli (1887–1969) was a commercial artist and industrial designer. As an artist he created posters and advertisements for Campari. After 1938 he worked for Olivetti, where he designed, for example, the adding machine Divisumma 14 (1947) and the typewriter Lettera 22.

The Castiglioni brothers' stool, Mezzadro (above) and Sgabello per Telefono (right), 1957 (reproduction by Zanotta), show the Italian wit and joy in experimentation. The Castiglioni brothers turned furniture into ready-mades.

Achille Castiglioni (1918–) studied architecture in Milan and worked since 1947 with his brothers, Pier Giacomo (1913–68) and Livio (1911–54), in their joint architecture office. He conducted important theoretical basic research for design and created innumerable designs for radios (Brionvega), lighting (Flos), furniture (Zanotta), and houshold items (Alessi). He was awarded the Compasso d'Oro several times and works today as a designer for international firms.

small, flexible, family enterprises was a prime force in molding the industry; from such a structure came a joy in experimentation that led to dynamic and individualistic forms. Thus, the abstract, dynamic forms of contemporary art became the model for chairs and tables. The motto for the 1951 Milan Triennale, which had been held since 1933 and later would become the most important exhibition for European designers, was "Unity of the Arts." The most noticeable example of the proximity between design and art was provided by Carlo Mollino. With his expressively curved furniture made of layered wood, Mollino became the representative of the organic style in Italy. In addition to furniture, he designed

Important Italian Furniture Companies of the 1950s

- Zanotta (f. 1954)
- Cappellini (f. 1946)
- Arflex (f. 1951)
- Kartell (f. 1949)
- Poltrona Frau (f. 1912)
- Cassina (f. 1927)
- Tecno (f. 1953)
- Molteni (f. 1933)

airplanes and racing cars, as well as architecture and erotic fashions. His organic furniture owes its expressively curved form to his preference for art nouveau (one of his great heroes was Gaudí) and his material of choice was bent plywood. This extreme organic style, however, never quite

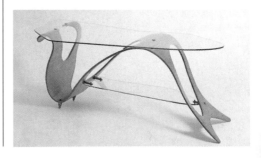

Carlo Mollino (1905–73), Arabesque Table from bent plywood with glass top, 1949.

1945 – 1960

managed to take hold in the designer's home country.

In furniture making, new materials were introduced with enthusiasm. Unlike such large automobile firms as Fiat or the typewriter manufacturer Olivetti, furniture companies tended to be small family firms, and it was exactly this that accounted for their flexibility. Firms like Kartell in Noviglio near Milan, for example, owed their success solely to their uncompromising openness to new man-made materials. Furthermore, like larger enterprises, the furniture manufacturers were quick to work with well-known architects and designers.

It was not only artistic individuality but also their openness to technical innovation—utility plus beauty—that made Italian design so famous in the ensuing decades, helped along by the proliferation of exhibitions, competitions, and magazines. In addition to the Milan Triennale, the Compasso d'Oro awarded annually since 1954 by the Milan store La Rinascente and the journals *Domus* (founded in 1928 by Gió Ponti) and *Casabello* (launched in 1929) supported Italian design economically and supplied it with a theoretical base. The journals discussed the newest European developments; the publishers themselves were always designers, even in later years.

Carlo Mollino, chair for the Casa Agra, 1955. (Reproduction by Zanotta.)

Gió Ponti, chair Superleggera, 1957, for Cassina. This chair became one of the best-known objects in Italy in the 1950s. Ponti (1891–1979), architect, designer, and author, took a more or less objective approach. In 1928 he founded the journal *Domus* and cofounded the Triennale in 1933. He created numerous designs for furniture, household wares, lighting, as well as stage settings and costumes for La Scala in Milan.

1945 – 1960

Osvaldo Borsani, chair P 40 with adjustable backrest, 1954, designed for Tecno.

"We're still sleeping on wire messes, and digging mines in latrines, and on top of them dreaming of summer houses, bowling alleys, turtledoves, of a refrigerator beautifully styled, of gargoyles: we're getting back to the Biedermeier."

Günter Grass, The Tin Drum, 1959

A German living room suite with upholstered furniture and coffee table, 1953.

1945 – 1960

Germany: From recovery to *Wirtschaftswunder*

During the years of Nazi domination, Germany was cut off from the international development of design and it sank into provincial small-mindedness. All the finest representatives of the Bauhaus had emigrated and industry had been either destroyed in the war, or dismantled. The postwar furniture industry, along with other sectors, had initially to improvise. First, the country's basic needs had to be met. The organizers of the first furniture fair after the war, held in 1949, still tried to model the exhibition on the patterns of the 1930s. Many of the furniture manufacturers considered themselves lucky if they had been able to hold onto their old plans and models. But the heavy upholstered furniture and daunting cabinetry of the prewar period were totally unsuited to the new environment. More than 5 million apartments had been destroyed in the war, and the most pressing task of design now lay in making arrangements for extremely small apartments with light, variable, multifunctional furniture that could be manufactured with a minimum of material and cost.

In the same year, the German Werkbund also organized an exhibition. The Werkbund en-

The "Gelsenkirch Baroque"—a combination living room and kitchen buffet with bar, 1956. This massive cabinet was manufactured in the 1930s without any consideration of the size of apartments or other apartment furnishings and continued to be produced after the war. Similar pieces still stand in countless worker apartments.

Joseph Caspar Ernst, poster for the 1949 Werkbund exhibition, "New Living" in Cologne.

Directions for building simple furniture from the Otto Maier publishing firm in Ravensburg, Germany.

gaged in the task of replacing the millions of lost homes and issued inexpensive, variable, and simple solutions for furnishing: practical folding beds, built-in cabinets, and light chairs for single-room apartments. In addition, they published patterns with directions for simple do-it-yourself furniture.

From the middle of the 1950s, as a growing taste for social display and ostentation accompanied the Wirtschaftswunder and people again looked to pseudo-historical furniture, these practical and simple pieces disappeared, at least from the homes of the upper classes.

Cabinet with a jalousie door (manufactured by R. Pfitzenmaier, Stuttgart). Such montage pieces were propagated by the German Werkbund after the war.

> "The market offers everything from pseudo-historical furniture to the expressly modern streamlined form."
>
> *Mia Seeger, 1953*

Industrie und Handwerk schaffen

neues Hausgerät in USA

Catalog for the exhibition, "Industry and Handwork Create New Household Equipment in the USA." American design was first presented after the war in 1951 in Stuttgart and established a new record with 60,000 visitors in a month.

The 1950s in Germany were not only the Swinging Fifties, but also a decade riddled with contradictions, of "Gelsenkirch Baroque," kidney-shaped tables, and neo-functionalism.

Kidney tables and melamine

The Marshall Plan was a coordinated effort by the United States and many European nations to foster European economic recovery after the Second World War. The United States dispensed more than $12 billion in aid, and with its share of this aid, Germany was able to begin in 1952–53 what would become known as the German *Wirtschaftswunder*, or economic miracle. Organic forms from the United States were enthusiastically adopted in Germany, and the borrowed style

> "Germany forgets about the gas chambers for a while, appears at the World's Fair with a smooth, elegant face, and acts as if technological progress justifies everything lying between a military tank and an electric razor."
>
> *Italian architect Bruno Zevi on the German entrant at the World Exhibit in Brussels, 1958.*

seemed to promise a new aesthetic orientation that would make it easier to repress the past without painful confrontation. The much quoted "zero hour" was declared. Life henceforth was colorful, optimistic, and full of the energy of a new beginning.

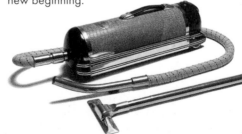

An Electrolux vacuum cleaner, 1950. (Design Museum, London)

The streamlined form, that sign of dynamism and progress, was applied to everything from baby carriages to vacuum cleaners. And the new materials and a hitherto unheard-of use of color made their way into many a living room. In addi-

> **Melamine**: a laminate, like formica. Laminates are usually made from layers of artificial materials glued together to cover furniture surfaces. They added durability, cleanability, and relative cost-effectiveness. In the 1950s and the 1980s they were often used to create colorful or patterned surfaces.

tion to conspicuously patterned wallpaper, curtains, and bar stools, laminated flower benches and other individual pieces conveyed the "modern" attitude of its owners. The kidney-shaped table became the symbol of an epoch.

"Good form"

Next to certain retrogressive tendencies and the influence from the United States, there were German designers who attempted to touch Germany's own historically unencumbered ideals from the prewar period. In Dessau, under Soviet occupation after the war, the Bauhaus was revived. In 1947 the German Werkbund was refounded and in 1951 in Darmstadt a Design Council was set up under the Ministry of the Economy; this council was close in spirit to the Werkbund and was supposed to support measures for the promotion of design. These design institutions were disciples of functionalism and rejected both organic forms and historicizing tendencies. The catch phrase for them was the

Typical wall lighting of the 1950s. Unusual materials such as punctured metal sheeting, brass piping, and gracefully shaped tube arms became a sign for a "modern" attitude.

1945 – 1960

A baby carriage from the 1950s. The streamlined form was carried over to a wide variety of everyday objects.

Chair from the firm Mauser, with a freely suspended bowl form. Modern art inspired wallpaper and upholstery patterns—not without leading to the unfortunate corollary—that modern art is only decoration.

term, "Good form." "Good," in the days of the Werkbund, referred to all that was aesthetically simple and functional, without superfluous decoration. In 1949 the term was borrowed for an exhibit by Max Bill in Ulm and Basel. Later in 1957 Bill published a book under the same name. "Good form" designated not merely an aesthetic, but at the same time a moral judgment, and remained a dogma of German design until well into the 1970s. "Good form" depended on simplicity, objectivity, durability, and through these, a timeless validity. The primary center promulgating these principles of "good form"—and it would continue to do so, exerting the most enduring influence on German design in the coming decades—was the Academy for Design in Ulm.

The Academy for Design

The most significant attempt in the 1950s to re-establish a connection with the democratic German design tradition of the 1920s and early 1930s, and to arrive at a modern and comprehensive design concept of its own was the Academy for Design in Ulm. Established by the Scholl Family Foundation in memory of Hans and Sophie Scholl, who had been executed by the Nazis for their activities in the resistance group "White Rose," the academy was explicitly anti-fascist, international, and democratically conceived. Students and teachers came from all over the world.

Max Bill (1908–94), painter, architect, designer, and theoretician, was a co-founder of the Academy for Design in Ulm, and until 1956 its first director. Bill thought of the Academy as a successor to the Bauhaus. With Hans Gugelot and Paul Hildinger, Bill designed the building (right, 1954), as well as the famous Ulm stool which became the symbol of the rational Ulm understanding. In 1957 he left the Academy in a dispute over its direction. He subsequently worked as a freelance designer for the watchmakers Junghans and Omega.

1945 – 1960

The Ulm Academy began teaching in 1953 and opened officially in 1955. Max Bill served as its first rector; Bill saw the school as a successor to the Bauhaus in its teaching methods, subject matter, and politics. He believed that design

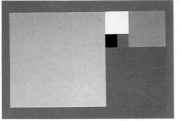

served a socially important role. The academy's first instructors were Otl Aicher, Hans Gugelot, and Tomás Maldonado. Walter Gropius deliv-

An example from the basic training of the Academy for Design: **Herbert Lindinger**, *Organization of Six Elements According to Principle*, 1954–56.

ered the opening address, arguing that "a broad education must point the right way for the right kind of cooperation between the artist, the scientist, and the businessman. Only together can they develop a product standard that takes man as the measure, that is, that takes the imponderables of our existence just as seriously as our physical needs. I believe in the growing importance of teamwork for the spiritualization of the standards of living in a democracy."

The structure of the Academy, like that of

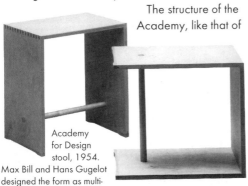

Academy for Design stool, 1954. Max Bill and Hans Gugelot designed the form as multifunctional furniture for academy students. It can also serve as a side table, a reading desk, and a bookcase.

Tomás Maldonado (1922–), industrial designer and theoretician, was appointed by Max Bill to the Academy for Design, Ulm, and worked there as an instructor (1954–67) and as director (1964–66). Maldonado held a technical-positivist position and effected the systematizing of modern design education. From 1968 to 1970 he held the chair for architecture at Princeton University, and from 1971 to 1983 at the University of Bologna, Italy.

The commercial artist and designer Otl Aicher (1922–91) was active in 1950 in the founding of the Ulm Academy for Design where he taught visual communication and was director from 1962 to 1964. In 1972 he took over the visual design of the Olympic Games in Munich (pictogram). Aicher created the corporate identity for such famous businesses as Braun, Erco, and BMW.

1945 – 1960

System thinking in product design: stackable hotel tableware, TC 100, by Hans Roericht for Rosenthal AG, 1958–59.

the Bauhaus, provided a basic foundation consisting of student collaboration in administration, group work, learning by doing, and theoretical "argumentation and the establishment of reasons for doing." The training was not oriented to individual subjects but was interdisciplinary. The academy was organized into four areas: product

The Foundations of the Academy for Design, Ulm
Philosophy: enlightenment, rationality, positivism
Methodology: Pestalozzi, Montessori, Kerschensteiner, Workers' School
Art and Design: Constructivism, De Stijl, Bauhaus

Hans Gugelot (1920–65), architect and industrial designer, worked as an architect with Max Bill and was appointed to the Academy for Design in Ulm in 1954, where he energetically expounded functionalism. Gugelot worked closely with industry, especially with Braun.

design, visual communication, building, and information, with an associated institute for filmmaking. The course lasted four years; after a general program in the first year, the student spent three years in one of the departments.

The academy expounded a functionalism based on simple rectangular forms, restrained coloration, and in particular, systematic thought. All the products designed at the academy were to serve an "autonomous use"—that is, to contribute to the education process itself in order to produce a socially conscious designer.

The school developed in several stages. The academy soon freed itself of the Bauhaus model and focused its education on the scientific, technological, and methodological fundamentals

1945 – 1960

Hans Gugelot, furniture system, M125, for Bofinger, Stuttgart, 1957. A furniture line in laminated sectional construction. The enlightened thinking of the Ulm Academy is manifest in furniture systems that were rationally produced and give the buyer the freedom to mix and match various elements.

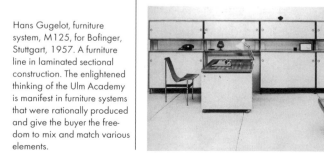

of design. Some of the teachers—especially Maldonado, Gugelot, and Aicher—completely rejected the role of art in design. Their position led to conflict with Max Bill and ultimately to his resignation.

At the beginning of the 1960s, strengthened under the new leadership of Tomás Maldonado (1964–66), the academy now shaped its program around purely technical problem solving. The design of furniture, lamps, and other ordinary household objects was no longer a concern; instead, the focus was on issues in the theory of information, and the academy turned to designing traffic and information systems.

The expression of systems thinking in architecture: cellular and slab structure with prefabricated cement sections. A student project under Herbert Ohl, 1961–62.

In its later years, near its eventual dissolution, under the direction of Herbert Ohl (1966–68), the academy worked increasingly in cooperation with firms such as Kodak and Braun. Industrial projects were supposed to provide the school with a strong practical orientation. But arguments over the direction of the academy led to problems for which no real solutions were forthcoming. Like the counterculture movement growing in

Hans Filbinger (1913–), a naval judge during the Third Reich and president of the German state of Baden-Wurttemberg from 1966 to 1978, declared at the closing of the Academy for Design in 1968, "We want to make something new, and to do that we must liquidate the old."

Visual communication: the symbol for Lufthansa was planned by Otl Aicher and Hans Roericht, among others, in conjunction with the airline. This design dates back to 1962–63. The Ulm designs are being further developed by Lufthansa today.

a number of countries, the reform movement that peaked in 1968 sharply criticized patterns of consumption and the role of design as a stooge of industry did not leave the Ulm Academy untouched. In addition, the school—a private institution—was subject to severe cuts in state funding, and was left in severe financial straits. The German legislature demanded that the school be joined with the public engineering school, but both the students and the faculty refused because they feared that such "nationalization" would endanger the academy's autonomy. Thus, the Ulm Academy was dissolved by the legislature of Baden-Württemberg under Governor Hans Filbinger.

The Ulm Academy for Design was adopted as a pattern for modern design education—known as the Ulm model—throughout the world. After its dissolution, its graduates were active in other institutions and important firms; it is through them that Ulm neo-functionalism became a design model for modern industrial products until well into the 1970s.

The high intellectual and moral ideals of the Ulm Academy remained incomprehensible to most consumers. Industry, however, adopted the systematic production philosophy of the academy because it became clear that the "building block" principle of construction allowed more rational production. The social critique at the heart of the Ulm methodology, of

Bruno Mathsson, arrangement of his summer house in Frösakull, Sweden, 1961.

1945 – 1960

course, was of little import to the larger industrial context.

Scandinavian home design

Next to the Italian joy in experimentation, American "styling," and German neo-functionalism, the 1950s and 1960s were known for the prominence of Scandinavian design.

Many pieces of Scandinavian furniture and Scandinavian commodities had been designed back in the 1930s, but did not become internationally known until after the war. Silver from Copenhagen and glass and ceramics by the Finnish firms Iitala and Arabia today remain an expression of open-minded bourgeois cultivation. At the 1951 Milan Triennale, Finnish products walked away with the most prizes.

Because industrialization came later to the Scandinavian countries than to Great Britain, the United States, or Germany, a relatively unbroken hand-craft tradition was still alive in furniture making even after the Second World War in Sweden, Finland, and Denmark. Wood had always been the building material of northern Europe. Now, not only were local birch and pine worked by the old techniques of the hand-craft tradition, but new methods of layering were also employed and organic forms created.

Arne Jacobsen, the chair, Ameise, designed in 1952 for the firm of Fritz Hansen, was the first mass-produced Danish chair. Today it comes in a range of colors.

1945 – 1960

Fritz Hansen, a Danish furniture company, was founded in 1872. The business was already famous in the 1930s because of the work of Kaare Klint. After the Second World War it produced furniture by Hans J. Wegner and specialized in modern techniques of forming wood and combinations with steel tube construction. By collaborating with well-known Scandinavian designers such as B. Arne Jacobsen, Poul Kjaerholm, and Verner Panton, Hansen became an important furniture manufacturer in the 1960s and 1970s. Today the firm still produces prize-winning chairs and office furniture.

Alvar Aalto, organically shaped vase for the firm of Iitala, 1930. This vase became internationally known after the war and is produced today in many variations.

After the war, the Danish furniture designers set the tone. Even before the war, Kaare Klint had arrived at organic forms based on a study of human proportions, and he became a model for the younger designers.

Hans J. Wegner's chair JH 501, the symbol of Scandinavian seating, later came to be known simply as "the Chair." It was made of teak, with a simple form and a woven seat; the Chair united uncompromising seating comfort with organically flowing transitions from the back to the armrests to the legs.

Teak takes hold

Denmark was the chief European importer of teak, which appeared on the world market in great quantities after the Indochinese War. The taste for teak also caught on in Germany, where light and practical Danish furniture suited the often cramped living quarters better than anything the German market had to offer. Moreover, the Scandinavian style, with its simple, bright, and friendly atmosphere, conveyed something of the democratic and humane understanding that stood behind it: after 1945 Sweden became the model social state. Scandinavian design was often found in the apartments and houses of the enlightened middle class. A veritable teak wave led in the following years to

Hans J. Wegner, chair, JH 501, a dining room chair from teakwood with a woven reed seat, 1949.

innumerable cheap imitations of Danish and Scandinavian furniture.

Danish modern

As new industrial production methods and materials were adopted in Denmark after the war, interesting connections arose between tradition and progress. The furniture was at once modern and comfortably homey—the main reason for the worldwide success of the Scandinavian furnishings—and it united the international style with a skilled craft tradition under the conditions of industrial production.

Like the American Arne Jacobsen bowl forms on tubing. His well-

Charles Eames, placed plywood frames of steel known chair

The Danish architect and designer Arne Jacobsen (1902–71) was one of the most important representatives of functionalism in the 1930s and 1950s. He worked in Copenhagen as a city planner, architect, and designer, and lived in exile in Sweden from 1943 to 1945. From 1956 to 1971 he was professor of architecture at the Academy in Copenhagen. Jacobsen designed several modern furniture classics for Fritz Hansen, including the chair Ameise (1952), chair model 3107 (1955), and the chair called The Egg (1957).

Poul Henningsen's hanging lamp, 1957, was a clean structure made of several simply arched plates. The lamp was functional and provided comfortable lighting without glare. It was widely copied.

Ameise was the first mass-produced Danish chair.

Danish designer Verner Panton was in many respects something of an outsider among Scandinavian designers: Panton was more influenced by what was happening in the United States and Italy, and worked less with wood than with steel wire and colorful plastics. For the use of such materials, he became a trailblazer in the 1960s and 1970s.

Verner Panton's ice cream cone chair, V-Chair 8800, designed for the firm of Fritz Hansen in the late 1950s, became a classic.

1945 – 1960

127

1957	First German nuclear reactor goes on line
1958	World's Fair in Brussels, Atomium
1961	The Berlin Wall is erected
1963	Assassination of President John F. Kennedy
1964	The Beatles make their first appearance on *The Ed Sullivan Show* on American television
1965	The United States sends troops to Vietnam
1966	High point of Minimal Art
1967	Marshall McLuhan, *The Medium Is the Message*
1968	Prague Spring; assassination of Martin Luther King in April and Robert F. Kennedy in June

1954 – 1968

Consumption and technology

If the 1950s were a time of new beginnings, the 1960s saw the peak of the economic miracle. In the intervening years, broad levels of society in the developed world participated in the prosperity and, after the period of reconstruction, technology was advancing rapidly: by the end of the decade, human beings—Neil Armstrong and Buzz Aldrin—had walked on the moon.

Technology and prosperity naturally had an influence on design and on the patterns of consumption in America and Europe. The number of electrical appliances, televisions, and stereos in every home increased steadily, more and more families owned automobiles, and home ownership grew. Design looked less toward traditional art and its trends than it had in the 1950s, and more toward technology, science, and methods of production.

Germany

The theory of functionalism so strongly represented by the Ulm Academy for Design, the orientation toward technology, and systems thinking all had their effect on mass production and brought about a rectangular formalism in both architecture and design, which was beginning to stimulate serious criticism of functionalism by the middle of the decade.

Verner Panton, futuristic home landscape at the "Visiona" during the Cologne Furniture Fair, 1970.

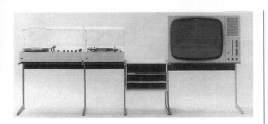

Dieter Rams, Combination phonograph-television, FS 600, by Braun, from the Ulm Academy systems design program, 1962–63.

Italy

The perennial Italian joy in experimentation, paired with a stronger export economy, transformed Italy into the leading design nation. In its work with synthetic materials in particular, Italy created the models for much of the new colorful, plastic furniture of the time. The larger manufacturers increasingly recognized the importance of design to their corporate image and began to collaborate with famous designers.

Design utopias

Advances in technology—in transportation, space exploration, communication, and even the processing of the new plastics—inspired designers to create futuristic worlds and to introduce products in new forms and colors.

At the end of the decade, protest mounted against encrusted social structures and the conspicuous consumption behavior of the affluent society. In design as well, political awareness grew, as consumer taste and designers' ideologies coalesced into a counterculture that stood against

The ultimate triumph of technology: in July 1969 Buzz Aldrin and Neil Armstrong were the first humans to set foot on the moon. Space technology and science fiction films influenced many design proposals.

1954 – 1968

mass consumption and against designers who functioned as industrial stooges. With the turn of the decade, design drew more

A demonstration in front of the America House in Stuttgart, 1969. Student unrest, demonstrations, alternative life-styles, youth subcultures, and rebellion against bourgeois consumer behavior influenced the design of the late 1960s and early 1970s.

129

"Good form": Timeless, glass design by Wilhelm Wagenfeld for WMF, Geislingen, Germany, 1950.

Wilhelm Wagenfeld (1900–90) was one of the fathers of modern industrial design in Germany and one of the leading exponents of the ideals of "good form." He studied with László Moholy-Nagy at the Bauhaus, and was first an assistant (from 1925) and later director (from 1929) of the Architecture Academy in Weimar. His simple and "timeless" forms found no argument with the Third Reich. In 1935 he became director of the United Upper Lausitz Glass Works, where he had already designed a stackable cubistic tableware system and glassware for mass production. After the war he worked as an instructor at the Academy of the Arts in Berlin and was a cofounder of the new Werkbund, and in 1957 cofounder of the journal Form. Before, during, and after the war, Wagenfeld worked for firms including the Jena Glass Works, WMF, Rosenthal, Thomas, Braun, Adler, and others. Many of his designs are still in production today, or are reproduced.

and more energy and ideas from the student movements, from pop art, pop music, and film.

"Good form" and neo-functionalism

The work of the Academy in Ulm had repercussions. The German design of the 1960s turned functionalism and "good form" into a stylistic principle that was often espoused with the force of dogma by institutions, design centers, and the Council for Design. Instructors at the academy worked for Braun, Vitsoe, Rosenthal, and others, whose products came to mean "good form" throughout the world. Functional and technical aspects of design assumed center stage and designers were more likely to think of themselves as engineers than as creators. In the face of this changing tide, the field of ergonomics emerged.

"Systems design" in architecture: the socially designed apartment building in the 1960s was marked by a false understanding of functionalism. Satellite towns on the edges of cities became mere bedroom communities connected to the cities by highways.

Even though the principles of the Academy for Design interested only an intellectual minority, the rectangular forms of the school's systems philosophy made their way into mass production,

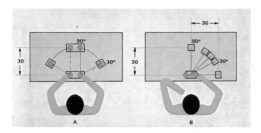

Ergonomics: the study of the patterns of movement in the workplace.

basically because the "building block" system facilitated inexpensive and "rational" production. The design and advertising lingo of various manufacturers began to sound more and more alike.

Shapes became harder, more angular, objective—but also less imaginative. A poor copy of functionalism, superficially quoting the rectangular form, led all too often to boring products or even to soulless satellite communities and cement slab settlements. The effect of this kind of urban, and suburban, community design varied from country to country, but more often than not, such attempts at convenient, but thoughtless design turned into trouble spots. Such

An integrated office workplace, 1970. The workplace should be fitted to the worker, and at the same time increase productivity.

1954 – 1968

"Good Form": Characterized by functionality, simple form, utility, durability, "timelessness," order, clarity, thorough and solid workmanship, suitable materials, finished details, technology, ergonomic design, environmental responsibility.
Ergonomics: Science of the relation between humans and their working conditions; concerned with seating that suits the human body and the shape of work equipment and its design in relation to the worker's movements. In industrial design in particular, ergonomics was at the center of design in the 1960s and 1970s.

The first Braun electric razor, S 50, 1950.

Manufacturer of stereos and household appliances, the Braun Corporation is the apotheosis of the Ulm Academy for Design. Since the 1950s, the company has worked with important functionalist designers including Hans Gugelot, Herbert Hirche, Dieter Rams, and Wilhelm Wagenfeld. The company became a model to many other companies on account of its clear, functional design as well as its exemplary, consistently modern corporate identity.

Founded in 1921 by M. Braun in Frankfurt, the company's initial venture was the production of components and parts for the still young radio industry. From 1929, Braun built its own radios and phonographs, and in 1936 it produced the first battery-operated transistor radio. During the Second World War, Braun held defense contracts for radio communication and electronic navigation systems.

After the war, the company broadened the range of its products. In 1950, it brought out its electric

Dieter Rams, tuner, TS 45, 1965. The rectangular shape, which can be combined with other components, boasts a simple, clear front with its arrangement of control knobs.

razor, the S 50. In 1951, Braun's sons expanded the firm's line to include kitchen appliances. Three years later, they hired Fritz Eichler as chief of design, who initiated a cooperative relationship with the Ulm Academy. With Hans Gugelot and Herbert Hirche, Eichler gave the firm its consistently modern stamp in everything from its business envelopes to its products to the architecture of its buildings.

Dieter Rams, who started working with Braun in 1955, finally carried the functional image of the firm to its peak with his motto, "Less Design Is More Design." Braun equipment under the influence of Rams was to be simple in form, comprehensible, and "timeless"—the tech-

Hans Gugelot and Dieter Rams, radio-phonograph combination, SK 4, 1956. Known as "Snow White's Casket," this radio-phonograph became an icon of modern design and today is a collector's item.

Braun reflects the taste of the times: the coffee machine Aromaster, 1985, was denigrated as a "postmodern misfire" because of its columnlike form and rippled back.

Milan in 1957 and 1960, as well as the Compasso d'Oro in 1962.

In spite of its claim of "timelessness," Braun has constantly adapted its products to the newest technical developments, and if one takes a close look, the accommodations to changing tastes are evident in every new model of electric razor or cappuccino machine.

The product range has been constantly broadened to include hair care equipment, travel irons, electric dental care systems and, in the 1980s, watches and alarm clocks. Braun invented, for example, voice and reflex control.

In 1990, Braun finally succumbed to the market pressures created by Japanese manufacturers and discontinued its line of hi-fi equipment. Limited editions of the last components it produced can be found today in the Museum of Modern Art.

nology must be perfect to the last detail.

Many of Braun's ideas were adopted by companies such as Siemens, AEG, Telefunken, Krups, and Rowenta—ideas such as compatibility of individual elements (the receiver, the turntable, the amplifier, and the cassette player), basic geometric forms, restrained use of color, and graphically designed fronts with easy-to-use controls. Braun products earned international respect and were awarded prizes at the triennial competitions in

The Braun Sixtant by Hans Gugelot, 1962, became a classic among modern electric razors.

Dieter Rams (1932–), chief designer as well as a member of the management team at Braun, is an outstanding representative of functionalism. From 1947 to 1953 he studied architecture and completed an apprenticeship in fine carpentry before working as an architect in Frankfurt in 1955. In the same year, he started working for Braun, where he became a product designer (1956), and eventually head of the design department (1961). Rams was closely related with the Academy in Ulm. With Hans Gugelot and Herbert Hirche, he designed Braun's corporate identity.

Richard Sapper (1932–), born in Munich, studied philosophy, commercial art, engineering science, and economics. Sapper worked from 1956 to 1958 at Mercedes Benz before moving to Italy, where he worked with Gió Ponti for the La Rinascente store and finally with Marco Zanuso for the hi-fi manufacturer Brionvega. In the 1970s and 1980s he designed famous lamps for Artemide and the water kettle "Bollitore" (1983) for Alessi. He also worked as an adviser for Fiat, Pirelli, and several furniture companies. Since 1986 he has been a professor at the Stuttgart Art Academy. Sapper has received the Compasso d'Oro a number of times.

low-income housing tended to be rejected utterly by communities in Great Britain, where they were often vandalized beyond habitability.

Italy: Bel design

Italy also experienced a period of prosperity and mass consumption in the 1960s. What became

Marco Zanuso and Richard Sapper, portable television, Aldol, for Brionvega, 1962.

known in Germany as "good form" in Italy was called "bel design," a concept that similarly ruled the mainstream design of the large manufacturers, and was also rational and production-oriented. But the Italian concept assigned design a different relative importance than did the German. Where equipment from Braun bore a sober model number such as *TS 45*, the Italian travel typewriter designed for Olivetti by Ettore Sottsass in 1969 was named *Valentine*. Similarly, the famous folding chair designed by Giancarlo

Marco Zanuso, folding radio, TS 502, for Brionvega, 1965.

Piretti was called *Plia*. These objects were fully imagined as idiosyncratic personalities, and were turned into symbols.

The second important characteristic of bel design was the implicit understanding of design as a part of culture. Large firms such as Olivetti or Fiat consciously worked with well-known designers; Italy virtually invented the profession of the "consultant designer" who freelanced as an adviser for a variety of companies. The idea of corporate identity assumed its own cultural dimension in Italy.

A great example of this holistic approach to design is Olivetti, who worked with young designers and architects such as Ettore Sottsass, Marco Zanuso, and Mario Bellini. Sottsass, who acted as consulting designer for Olivetti's then-new electronics department from 1958 to 1960,

Mario Bellini (1935–) is one of the most influential Italian designers. He studied architecture at the Milan Polytechnic and then founded an architecture and design office. Since 1963 he has worked as a consultant designer for Olivetti and for such companies as B&B Italia, Cassina, Lamy, Brionvega, Artemide, and many others. Between 1962 and 1971, he received the Compasso d'Oro six times. In 1987 the Museum of Modern Art presented a one-man show of his work.

The folding chair, Plia, 1969, by Giancarlo Piretti is the archtype for any number of folding chairs produced by various manufacturers today.

was not only responsible for the notably functional design of new computers, but also headed his own department for "cultural relations " and publicity, and conferred directly with the management. With this open attitude, design at Olivetti soon became an important component of company policy.

Design, moreover, was not a matter only for specialists and engineers, but also engaged architects, philosophers, and writers.

1954 – 1968

Ettore Sottsass and Perry A. King, the portable typewriter, *Valentine*, with case, for Olivetti, 1969.

135

Mario Bellini, electric calculator, Divisumma 18, for Olivetti, 1972.

The great theoreticians of Italian design—Gillo Dorfles, Giulio Carlo Argan, Vittorio Gregotti, and Umberto Eco—carried on, as they do today, public discussions about design in the proliferating numbers of journals of architecture and design.

The third characteristic of Italian design, the joy in experimentation, thrived in the environment of almost unlimited design possibilities design offered by the new synthetics. Italy became the leader in design development. Its position was clearly stated in a 1972 exhibition, "Italy: The New Domestic Landscape," at the Museum of Modern Art. The exhibit catalog, which has become a collector's item worth several hundred dollars, made it clear to the entire world that the Italian hegemony in design was uncontested. At the exhibition, mainstream and antidesign, the elegant and the experimental, the classical and the provocative could be seen side by side. The exhibition embodied the tolerance and openness that characterize Italian design to this day.

Richard Sapper, low-voltage halogen lamp, Tizio, for Artemide, 1972. In its carefully thought-out functionalism, the lamp resembles German designs of the 1960s and 1970s, but has been transformed by Italian elegance. In the 1980s, the lamp became an icon of advanced lighting.

1954 – 1968

Exhibition catalog, *Italy: The New Domestic Landscape*, Museum of Modern Art, New York, 1972. The individual objects seen on the cover are movable behind a sheet of parchment.

Plastics and polyesters

Even in the early days of Bakelite, man-made materials were a hallmark of modern design. In Italy, enthusiasm for the modern, as for plastics, was always strong.

Around 1952, the Italian Giulio Natta, with Karl Ziegler, invented polypropylene. For this remarkable achievement, they were awarded the Nobel prize for chemistry in 1963. This invention was to revolutionize furniture making. Finally, durable chairs and tables in all possible forms could be made inexpensively by a machine at a single stroke.

Verner Panton (1926–), Danish architect and designer, created probably the best-known all-plastic chair of the 1960s. After his studies in Copenhagen, he first worked for Arne Jacobsen and then moved to Switzerland in 1955. In the same year, he designed his Side Chair, a free-swinging chair made out of fiberglass-reinforced polyester. The chair was first produced by the firm of Herman Miller in 1968.

New Man-Made Materials in Furniture Construction

Polypropylene, Polyurethane, Polyester, Polystyrol
Advantages: Furniture can be produced entirely by machine in any color; these materials are fully malleable, light, cheap, and "modern."

By now, many manufacturers were working intensely on the further development of foam materials, nylon, and polyester. Experience from war-time production was transferred to everyday items, and the chemical industry searched constantly for new uses for the improved synthetics. One such use was found in the area of household wares and furniture production.

Kartell

In the aftermath of the Second World War, a new array of companies was established, initially concerned with manufacturing household goods. These companies brought colorful plastic containers, tableware, and other items to the market. One such new firm was Kartell, founded in 1949 by the chemist Giulio Castelli in Milan. Initially, Kartell produced synthetic automobile parts, but since the middle of the 1950s it was

1954 – 1968

Verner Panton, Side Chair (also called the Panton Chair), 1968. Panton had designed the chair in 1959 or 1960, but it was produced as late as 1968.

In Germany, too, furniture designers in the 1960s worked with man-made materials. Helmut Bätzner's stackable chair dates from 1966.

Joe Colombo (1930–71) was one of the outstanding designers of the 1960s and the "Master of Plastic Design"—his futuristic shapes were inspired by space travel and the science fiction of the 1960s.

primarily concerned with the development and production of household wares. In the 1960s Kartell turned to lamps and furniture and became the industry leader in the field of plastic design. Kartell's company policy, aside from its openness to new technology and willingness to experiment with new designs, was distinguished by its practice of always working with well-known designers. Under the advisory and artistic direction of the architect and designer Anna Castelli-Ferrieri, Kartell has constantly experimented since 1966 with new synthetic combinations, not only to enhance the beauty and durability of its furniture, but also to control, or even decrease, the cost for the customer. Among the company's most popular products are the children's high chair by Marco Zanuso and Richard Sapper (1964), the stackable chair 4860 by Joe Colombo, and the plastic container designed by Anna Castelli-Ferrieri herself. In the 1980s Kartell also produced plastic furniture by Philippe

Joe Colombo's stackable plastic chair, 4860, for Kartell. The hole in the back was purely functional: it made it easier to remove the chair from its mold.

Starck, Matteo Thun, Michele de Lucchi, and others.

Questions of image

The plastic wave reached both a high point and a crucial turning point with the oil crisis of 1973. From that point, plastic was no longer glamorized as "modern" and "high-tech," it was spurned as "cheap," tacky, tasteless, and—with the growing environmental awareness—unecological. For furniture, it was deemed suitable mainly for outdoor use, say, as garden furniture, or for commercial and public areas.

It was precisely this image as "cheap" and "ordinary" that led the "Memphis" group, and later representatives of the New Design—with their preference for the objects of daily life, for plastic laminates and glaring colors—to attempt to rehabilitate the previously scorned material and to bring it back inside, into private living quarters in the early 1980s.

Joe Colombo's rolling cart, Baby, plastic, 1970, created for Bieffeplast, is still a favorite today with architects and commercial artists.

1954 – 1968

Today the colorful plastic furniture of the 1960s and 1970s fetches astonishing prices as collectors' items at auctions. Bonham's in London is considered the leading auction house for design.

1964   The Rolling Stones release their first album

1966   Susan Sontag, *Against Interpretation*; Andy Warhol's series of electric chairs

1968   Stanley Kubrick, *2001: A Space Odyssey*

1969   Woodstock Music Festival

1970   Pop stars Jimi Hendrix and Janis Joplin die

1972   A break-in at the Watergate Hotel in Washington, D.C. launches investigations of Richard Nixon's presidency (he resigns in 1974); Francis Ford Coppola's *The Godfather* wins the Academy Award

1975   Baader-Meinhof trial begins

1976   Founding of the "Alchimia" group; Jimmy Carter is elected president

1978   The popularity of disco reaches a peak with the movie *Saturday Night Fever*

1965 – 1976

Experimentation, utopia, and antidesign

Despite the apparent blossoming of the consumer society and the popularity of a spurious brand of functionalism toward the latter half of the 1960s, the handwriting was already on the wall. Economies, it seemed, had reached the limits of growth, or, at the very least, of the fast-paced growth to which they had become accustomed. And then with the early 1970s came the oil crisis of 1973. The crisis, brought on by an OPEC decision to raise oil prices dramatically, meant oil shortages, inflation, and other problems for the oil-importing nations. OPEC's decision also brought on a general sense of economic and ecological vulnerability that filtered down into most walks of life.

The consumer society takes a hit

The euphoric atmosphere surrounding mass production and the purely purposive rationalism of modern design were now increasingly attacked, while the role of design in a capitalistic society was loudly questioned. Not all designers wanted either to be, or to be perceived as, pawns of industry, perpetuating value systems that no longer

Peace, love, and understanding: The Woodstock festival in upstate New York is the crowning glory of the American counterculture.

served a useful purpose. They chose instead to work independently and experimentally for themselves. Many stepped into the arena of political statement and incorporated over-arching social concepts in their work. The protests against the war in Vietnam, the Prague Spring, the student unrest in the cities of Europe and America were felt in all spheres of life. In the early 1970s, a body of critical theory about design called into question its task in society.

Pop design of the 1960s. The background uses a decoration from a motif by Roy Lichtenstein.

The crisis of functionalism

Functionalist theory offered no clear answer to this question. Aesthetic models were sought in areas apparently unrelated to design. The counterculture, rock music, young people, pop art, movies not just from Hollywood but from countries around the world—all contributed to a new perspective on the nature of design. Radical countermovements against functionalist architecture as well as against the dominance of mainstream industry and design institutions sprang up first in England, then in Italy and Germany. The United States made its first attempts to take a critical view of modernism and focused on the cultural, psychological, and symbolic underpinnings of architecture, leading to the first formulations of postmodernism.

"The inadequacy of the purely purpose-oriented form is revealed for what it is—a monotonous, impoverished boring practicality."
Theodor W. Adorno

1965 – 1976

Oliver Morgue, Living Model 1972 at "Visiona," the exhibit by Bayer Leverkusen at the Cologne Furniture Fair. Anti-authoritarian attitude and futuristic visions led to open "democratic" living areas, so-called living landscapes.

Detail of an apartment house built in the 1960s.

The German critique of functionalism

In Germany, where functionalism in architecture and design had been so doggedly preached since the war, and where large new settlements on the edges of cities yielded unanticipated negative results (in the form of crime, vandalism, etc), the mid-1960s gave rise to debates in architecture and city planning over the emotional deficits of objective rationalism oriented exclusively toward rationalized mass production. Even the role of the arts in the designing process—a role always rejected by the functionalists—was drawn into the fray.

The climax of the discussion was a lecture by Theodor Adorno, "Functionalism Today," delivered before the German Werkbund in 1965. Adorno criticized the puritanical principles of the functionalists as ideologically excessive; moreover, functionalism, claimed Adorno, had produced "hardly a form that was not a symbol in addition to its fitness for utility." The architect Wolfgang Nehls demanded in 1968 that "the sacred cows of functionalism ... be sacrificed." Nehls condemned the inhuman formalism of the concrete slab apartment complexes of the 1960s and 1970s: "What is criminal is that the principles of clarity and severity have led us to a poverty of design." Alexander Mitscherlich noted the "inhospitality of our cities." A pointed political criticism of the role of design in the capitalistic economic

Bremen-Vahr, 1959, a satellite community designed by architect Alvar Aalto according to the principles of the "bedroom community," where access to the city center via public transportation and highways was a primary design factor.

system came from Wolfgang Fritz Haug's *Critique of Product Aesthetics*. Haug criticized designs that actually detracted from a product's utility and seduced the consumer into purchasing a product he or she may not need—or that may not have been the best available—with a superficial glitter that has little to do with the usefulness of the product and everything to do with the need of the market to stimulate sales—in short, "styling."

Ingo Maurer, lamps in the shape of oversized light bulbs, 1966–68 reveal an interplay of function and symbol.

Alternative design

The various social critiques of design came mainly in public, verbal forums; they remained in the realm of theory and had little actual impact on industrial design. Nonetheless, individual designers were motivated either by their agreement with such positions, or from the promptings of their own consciences, to develop alternative concepts

Des-in, tire-sofa, 1974. Here principles of recycling are translated into alternative design.

which in the early 1970s reflected a growing consciousness of the limits of the industrial society. The Great Society of the 1960s, the society that saw unlimited progress and put man on the moon—even in the face of growing social unrest and political as well as personal violence—was limited by a finite reserve of raw materials, by the adverse byproducts of industrialization such as pollution and ozone depletion, and by any number of other social and environmental factors.

1965 – 1976

143

1966. The miniskirt by English fashion designer Mary Quant spread throughout the world (generations later, people would wonder who really preferred the style, and for whom it was really designed—men or women). The fabric shown here is a typical "flower-power" print.

Carla Scolari, Donato D'Urbino, Paolo Lomazzi and Gionatan de Pas, inflatable chair, Blow, 1967. At the end of the 1960s, furniture made from polyvinyl chloride (PVC) became stylish as the essence of youthfulness and flexibility.

Thus, in 1974 Jochen Gros and the group "Des-in" tried to implement recycling design and alternative methods of design, production, and sales. Printers' plates became lampshades, tea boxes turned into closets, car tires became sofas. Munich designer Ingo Maurer reconsidered the function of lamps. His experimental projects were not economically feasible at that time, and at first had little impact on the industrial design of the large companies, but they paved the way to a new understanding, not only among designers and manufacturers but among users as well. One outcome of Maurer's innovations was a do-it-yourself wave.

Pop culture and utopias

Alternatives to the vehemently criticized functionalism came increasingly from the youth culture of

the 1960s. From British and American pop music and the commercial adoption of the hippie movement came the language and culture of "flower power," which, together with pop art, influenced commercial art, fashion, and the experimental furniture of a number of designers. The youth culture of the 1960s represented a revolt against traditional behavior patterns, while pop art represented a rebellion against aesthetic norms. The banal objects of daily life (e.g., soup cans, hamburgers), comics, and advertisements simultaneously stood as art and as a parody of the consumer society in the pictures of Roy Lichtenstein, Claus Oldenburg, and Andy Warhol.

This new aesthetic reached the sphere of the designers. The synthetic materials allowed play-

Joe Colombo, Central Living Blocks at "Visiona," 1969. Inspired by science fiction, outer space utopias, these designs feature an open living area with couch and a dining area with plastic furniture.

ful, often ironic and provocative forms, and in connection with the revolt of the 1968 generation against the conventional middle-class lifestyle, alternative models of living were explored. Kitsch, camp, and the culture of everyday life moved back into the apartment, in a wave of nostalgia with a taste for the exotic, for the disposable, and the prefab.

Counterculture, of course, was not the only aesthetic influence on the 1970s. The combination of man's actual experiences in space exploration and the popular visions of science fiction films suggested infinite technical possibilities. Stanley Kubrick's 1968 cult film *2001: A Space Odyssey* inspired designers to create futuristic living worlds. (Kubrick clearly liked to experiment with futuristic designs, though not always with such

1965 – 1976

Guido Drocco and Franco Mello, Cactus, clothes stand, 1971. Shapes taken from comic books made from the new foam were also turned into furniture.

Piero Gatti, Franco Teodoro and Cesare Paolini, Sacco, 1968–69. The beanbag chair, a sack filled with polystyrene pellets, was supposed to fit itself to every body shape and sitting position. It was therefore the epitome of a relaxed and antiauthoritarian style of living. Actually, by the 1970s, the widely popular chair proved to be rather uncomfortable.

Furniture for sitting and lying, Pratone (large meadow) by Strum, 1971, was one of the best-known examples of antidesign. It looked discouragingly hard, but was in reality soft and comfortable. Irony and playfulness were greatly beloved by the antidesign movement.

1965 – 1976

a healthy and peaceful-feeling tone: the future world he created in his later film, *A Clockwork Orange*, might be considered as expressive of the same aesthetic vision as the earlier film, but with a far more horrific undercurrent.) Centralized housing communities equipped with everything necessary for both technical and psychosocial functioning, like those one might imagine aboard a space ship—even the camp futuristic automated possibilities suggested by popular television shows like *Star Trek* and even *The Jetsons*—were supposed to reform the image of the dwelling unit. The outline of the living area was open, the furniture was plastic. Appliances were designed to assume more automated tasks—ice makers, can openers, self-cleaning ovens, self-defrosting refrigerators. Unlike the angular "rational" functionalism, such new worlds of living spoke to people's emotional and sensual needs.

Unlike the ecological or socially critical approaches, positive utopia visions were more or less silenced by the 1973 oil crisis. Outsiders to design such as Luigi Colani, who gained respect as well as criticism with his organic forms in plastic and his visionary designs, were dismissed by design institutions as exotics, or were not noticed at all.

Italian countermovements

Italian design had always been characterized not only by cultural awareness, but by philosophical, political, and socially critical consciousness. Now, toward the end of the 1960s, a new generation of Italian architects and designers were feeling dissatisfied with educational and working conditions and with the consumption-oriented bel design of industrial products. They no longer wanted to design elegant single pieces, but to look with fresh eyes at the design process, with full consideration of the political conditions in the con-

New New York, 1969. The group Superstudio laid a geometric gridwork over cities and objects to offer a new grasp of things from a "neutral" point of view.

sumer society. The main centers of "radical design" were Milan, Florence, and Turin, where designers organized themselves into groups in order to work up a radical comprehensive jumping-off point for the generation of principles for human existence. The protest against established design and the fetishes of consumption and objects was expressed primarily in drawings, photo montages, and utopian projects. Concrete objects were less of a focus. As father of the countermovement, Ettore Sottsass had already adopted the forms of pop art and proposed utopian counterworlds.

One of the earliest antidesign groups was "Archizoom," founded in Florence in 1966, with Andrea Branzi and Paolo Deganello. Archizoom's theoretical writings on architecture and city planning were particularly hostile toward the use of the elegant design as a status symbol. Another group, "Strum," wanted to use architecture and design for political propaganda. The critical position of many antidesignists developed into a growing pessimism and operated on the principle of the complete avoidance of every possible object. This gloomy attitude persisted into the 1970s and many designers, including Sottsass, ceased to produce any practical design work at all, confining themselves to self-expression in theory and in drawings. By the middle of the 1970s most of the countermovements had dissolved or disbanded, and Italian avant-garde design stagnated in uncertainty until the beginning of the 1980s.

Oversized ceramics by Ettore Sottsass, a central figure of Italian antidesign, 1967. These columns were inspired by pop art, but because of cultural associations, were realized in ceramic.

Representatives of Radical Design

- *Superstudio,* Milan, 1966
- *Archizoom Associati,* Florence, 1966
- *Gruppo 9999,* Florence, 1967
- *Gruppo Strum,* Turin, 1966
- *Global Tools,* Milan, 1973
- *Alchimia,* Milan, 1976

1965 – 1976

1978	Charles Jencks, *The Language of Postmodern Architecture*; Exhibition "The New Wild Ones" at the Maenz Gallery in Cologne
1979	Birth of the Sony Walkman
1981	The cable television station MTV airs music videos round the clock
1982	Umberto Eco, *The Name of the Rose*
1983	The film, *Wild Style*, features break dancing and rap music; Spiegel's first report on AIDS
1984	Fritjof Capra's book *Turning Point* popularizes the term "New Age"
1986	Disaster at the Chernobyl Nuclear Power Plant in Ukraine
1988	George Bush is elected president
1989	Dismantling of the Berlin Wall
1990	U.S. space probe Magellan returns a radar map of Venus
1991	Dissolution of the Soviet Union; Persian Gulf War
1992	Bill Clinton elected president; the Maastricht Treaty strengthens the European Community
1994	Opening of the "Chunnel" under the English Channel, connecting England and France

1968 – present

A 1970s living room: "Good taste" was now expressed in confident combinations of various styles.

148

From modern to postmodern

Radical antidesign movements aroused considerable media attention at the end of the 1960s, but most of them disappeared within a few years without ever achieving much success. Socially critical pop furniture was at first a mere fashionable accessory. In Germany, where the "Federal Prize for Good Form" continued to be awarded annually, the utopias of the countermovement proved weaker than the structures of the industrial society.

Among consumers, however, the diverse new aesthetic influences of the 1970s generated a broad spectrum of tastes, creating an environment marked by a flood of different life-styles all contradicting and negating the solipsistic claims of "good form" and functionalism. This pluralism was a social phenomenon. In the late 1970s and 1980s the simple divisions of working class, middle class, and upper class were no longer adequate to describe the complicated sociological structure of the modern industrial countries.

Taste and style among the different segments of the population of the developed nations had grown so various that it was no simple matter to distinguish, as functionalism had tried to do, between "good" and "bad."

Out of an awareness of the various worlds of taste open to any individual grew an awareness of the emotional insufficiency of functionalism and of the multiplicity of functions an object may perform;

The Notch Project, Sacramento, California, 1976–77. Postmodern play with meaning and perception. The American architect group SITE interpreted the entrance to a Best store by "breaking open" the building.

The AT&T Building in New York, by Philip Johnson, 1978–82, sparked lively discussion among architects and theoreticians.

this generated an opposition to modernism that questioned the prevailing standards. Postmodernism, an ambiguous term, was often used in an inflated manner in the heated debates of the 1980s—and just as often invoked for polemical purposes. The postmodern countermovement first became manifest in architecture, as a less political, but more successful endeavor than the earlier radical movements. The most obvious characteristic of the postmodern, the reference to and combination of historical stylistic "quotations," constitutes the chief bone of contention between pro-postmodernists and anti-postmodernists.

Postmodern theory

Toward the end of the 1960s, partly stimulated by pop culture, the first attempts appeared in various cultural spheres to reject the divisions into "good" and "bad," into "good form" and "kitsch," into "high culture" and "popular culture." Even the fundamental relationship between form and function was no longer automatically accepted. The postmodern rebelled with its use of historical citations, camp and pomp, individuality and colorfulness against the colorless rational forms of a dogmatic modernism. The expression "postmodern" had appeared back in the 19th century, and in a narrower sense in the literary criticism of the early 1960s. It was not until the 1980s that it was

Contributors to the Postmodern
Leslie Fiedler, Charles Jencks, Robert Venturi, Umberto Eco, Heinrich Klotz, Jürgen Habermas, Jean Baudrillard, Jean-François Lyotard, Jacques Derrida, Peter Sloterdijk, Achille Bonito Oliva, Wolfgang Welsch, and others

1968 – present

Architects of the Postmodern
Michael Graves, Hans Hollein, Rob Krier, Aldo Rossi, Robert Venturi, Charles Moore, James Stirling, Philip Johnson, Helmut Jahn, Ricardo Bofill, Gottfried Böhm, and others

applied to architecture and in the social sciences and liberal arts. In philosophy, "postmodernism" first occurs around 1979, and discussion involving the term seemed to climax in the 1980s.

Postmodern architecture
The American Robert Venturi formulated antifunctionalist theses in his books *Complexities and Con-*

Charles Moore's Piazza d'Italia in New Orleans, 1975–80, is the essence of postmodern architecture.

traditions in Modern Architecture (1966) and *Learning from Las Vegas* (1971). The symbolic suggestions of commercial buildings and billboards in Las Vegas launched a reevaluation of the function of buildings. It was at that point that Charles Jencks first applied the term "postmodern" to architecture. The hallmark of the

"Every object is also a symbol."
Roland Barthes

Hans Hollein, the Marilyn sofa, 1981. Rare woods and upholstery fabrics are common to many postmodern furniture designs.

postmodern building is the historical reference to style; these buildings make use of decorative, sign-like, symbol-like elements, often with an underlying suggestion of irony or humor. The postmodern seeks in such ways to speak to the observer.

Postmodern design

Design soon borrowed the term postmodern from architecture, though often in a constricted sense applied to furniture and other things that generally cited architectural forms. In fact, however, a number of different characteristics comprised postmodern design, including colorful and signlike shaping of surfaces (which had by now become totally independent of function), the reinterpretation of an object's appearance in relation to its use, and again, as in postmodern architecture, the quotation and combination of historical elements. At the same time, taking a stand that went directly against the grain of functionalistic doctrine, postmodern designers combined rich ornamentation with minimalist forms, expensive materials with kitsch. Formally, postmodernism in the 1970s and 1980s was above all a blow for freedom from the dictates of the modern; structurally, the new movement was influenced by the rapid incursion of microelectronics into every area of life, and the resulting restructuring of industry and society.

"Studio Alchimia"

It is generally agreed that the first objects of postmodern design were furniture issued by the Italian groups Alchimia and Memphis.

In 1976, Alessandro Guerriero founded the Studio Alchimia in Milan, with theoretical leadership provided by Alessandro Mendini. The studio's philosophy was in every respect the opposite of the objective and technical product orientation of functionalism. The roots of the group lay in the radical movement of the 1960s, but Alchimia defined itself

Michael Graves, dressing table, Plaza, 1981, for Memphis. Much postmodern furniture imitates architectural forms, such as skyscrapers.

A tea kettle from Alessi (1985) by Michael Graves became one of the most popular designer objects of the postmodern period.

Members of the Alchimia Group
Alessandro Guerriero, Alessandro Mendini, Andrea Branzi, Ettore Sottsass, Michele de Lucchi, Ugo La Pietra, Trix Haussmann, Robert Haussmann, Riccardo Dalisi, and others

1968 – present

Distortion of Great Works, 1978; Alessandro Mendini's redesigns of modern classics, here Gerrit Rietveld's chair, Zig-Zag, questioned traditional expressions of design.

as a "postradical forum of discussion," because it took no political position. The goal was to produce a new emotional and sensual relationship between user and object, as opposed to the indifferent functionality of modern mass products. As a result, the group did not seek to mass-produce its designs, nor was it deeply concerned with the objects' utility. Instead, Alchimia designers focused on the ability to radiate the expressive, the witty and imaginative, the poetic and the ironic.

The name "Alchimia" is a whimsical reference to medieval alchemy, which was the "science" of turning ordinary substances into gold. The Group Alchimia reworked "cheap" everyday commodities with glaring colors and superimposed ornaments to create "golden" objects of design.

Another approach was redesign, the formal reworking of classics of modern design. Well-known objects from the Glasgow School to the Bauhaus chair were "de-

Alessandro Mendini (1931–) studied architecture in Milan and works with Nizzoli as a designer. Mendini was one of the theoreticians of Italian antidesign, a cofounder of the group Global Tools in 1973, editor-in-chief of the journal *Casabella* from 1970 to 1975, and publisher of *Domus* from 1979 to 1985. With Alessandro Guerriero, he founded the Studio Alchimia in 1976 where he developed his philosophy of redesign and commonplace design. After the disbanding of Alchimia, he produced designs for Alessi, Swatch, Rasch, Vitra, and many other companies.

Studio Alchimia, Unfinished Furniture, with magnetic appliqués, 1981: furniture as collage.

corated" with little flags, bright appliqués, balls, and other ornaments; the effect was an ironical admixture of antithetical elements.

Studio Alchimia, redesign of commonplace objects with colored arrows, flags, etc., 1980.

Alchimia presented its work to the public through drawings, exhibitions, and performances. In so doing, they presented poetic architectural designs, costumes, videos, and stage sets. In 1979 they introduced the first "Bauhaus Collection"; in 1981 the "I Mobili infiniti" (Unfinished Furniture) project. Around 30 designers, artists, and architects designed individual pieces—handles, legs, casters—that could be combined at will. Colorful decorations were attached with magnets. Combining extremely different, even discordant forms, colors, and materials became a kind of governing principle; a piece of furniture was understood as a three-dimensional collage. The primary value of these objects lay not in the solution of functional problems, but in the staging of sensual appearances. Among the artists participating in the I Mobili infiniti project were Francesco Clemente, Mimmo Paladino, and Sandro Chia.

At the beginning of the 1980s Studio Alchimia was the most important design group on the international scene. It participated in many exhibits, including the trailblazing 1980 Forum Design held in Linz, Austria. In 1981 Ettore Sottsass left Alchimia to cofound the Memphis group.

"Memphis"
The Memphis group splintered from Studio Alchimia in 1981. Ettore Sottsass, Andrea Branzi, Michele de Lucchi, and others left Alchimia because

Bookcover for *Memphis, The New International Style*, Electa Publishers, 1981.

1968 – present

153

Ettore Sottsass Jr. (1917–) is one of the most interesting and influential contemporary designers. He studied architecture in Turin, founded a studio for architecture and design in Milan in 1947, and worked with George Nelson in New York in 1956. In 1958 he moved to Olivetti where he was a consulting designer until 1980. In addition to his professional activities, Sottsass became a leader of Italian antidesign. He was a cofounder of Global Tools, Alchimia, and Memphis, and in 1980 founded Sottsass Associates, which is active today in a wide range of design areas; they produce designs for Cassina, Mitsubishi, Alessi, Coca-Cola, and Olivetti. After the end of Memphis, Sottsass turned his attention to architecture.

they found the intellectual approach of Alessandro Mendini and the handcrafted character of Alchimia's products too depressing. The Memphis group preferred to place its focus on the sensual relationship between object and user and wanted to extend their work further than manifestos, ideal communities, and individually provocative pieces as a radical antidote to functionalism. The Memphis designers, unlike those of Alchimia, were all in favor of industry, advertising, and the practical aspects of daily life. They found the rapid changes in fashion in the postmodern society a source of inspiration, and Memphis furniture was expressly designed for mass production.

For Memphis, ordinary daily things were the particular characteristics of contemporary life. Thus, they transplanted the colorful plastic laminates (melamine, formica) from the bars and cafés of the 1950s and 1960s into the private resi-

> Many internationally known architects and designers worked for the Memphis studio, in addition to Ettore Sottsass, Andrea Branzi, and Michele de Lucchi—Matteo Thun, Michael Graves, Arata Isozaki, Shiro Kuramata, Javier Mariscal, Natalie du Pasquier, Hans Hollein, and others. The theoretician and chronicler of the studio was Barbara Radice.

dence. These resins, a "metaphor for vulgarity, poverty, and bad taste," were stylized into a work-a-day mythos and declared a statement—newly laden with meaning. Memphis derived their ideal home decorations from daily life: from comic strips, movies, punk music, screaming in sweet pastel colors, playful, symbolic, and witty. Their intention was

Martine Bedin, Super lamp, 1981. Many of the Memphis objects were inspired by children's toys; they are colorful, cheerful, and playful.

to excite a form of spontaneous communication between object and user. The practical purpose of the objects was of no concern.

Like the patterns on the surface of objects, materials such as glass, steel, industrial sheet metal, and aluminum were brought together to suggest new meaning. Many items resembled children's toys or

»Superior«   »Ontario«   »Michigan«

took their cue from exotic cultures. Memphis produced collages whose main purpose was decorative, and whose principle was chaos. In all, the Memphis designers saw a parallel to the splintering, disconnectedness, and mobility of the postmodern world.

Memphis also readily took up the tools of sociology and marketing: though they had no intention of supplying products for the mass market, they did aim to reach "certain segments of cultural groups with various languages, traditions, and patterns of behavior." The movement introduced a basically new understanding of design, from both an aesthetic and a conceptual perspective, so much so that today one can speak of pre- and post-Memphis design and thinking. The group inspired many developments in the New Design of the 1980s, though it also provided the model for many lesser imitations. Toward the end of the decade, with the appearance of

"Today we use up everything that we make. Our products are devoted to life, not posterity."

Ettore Sottsass

Matteo Thun, salt-and-pepper shakers, 1982, for the Memphis group.

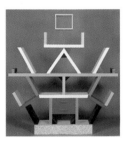

Ettore Sottsass, Carlton shelves, 1981. Mythical symbols and colorful plastic laminate make furntiture into a communicative object.

Peter Shire, the Bel Air chair, 1982, for Memphis.

1968 – present

155

"Punk, luxury, ethnos, microelectronics, ecology, the new modesty, apocalyptic fears, hedonism—all this and more are the ingredients of the bubbling kettle of design that spit forth an endless flood of objects from superficial fashion knickknacks to intelligently thought-out and imaginatively carried out innovations."

Albrecht Bangert, 1991.

a flood of shrill and strange forms and colors, the influence of Memphis diminished.

The "wild eighties"

In the 1980s technical, social, ecological, and cultural developments, as well as those in style, accelerated to such an extent and so radically that this decade stands

Gaetano Pesce, Green Street Chair, 1984/86/87 (made by Vitra).

out against the backdrop of those that went before. Just as art had turned away from the conceptual phases of the 1960s and 1970s toward an expressive, figured "wild" painting, so architecture and design finally turned away from the dogmas of modernism and functionalism.

The effect of the Memphis group on this transition can hardly be overstated; another essential turning point was the "Forum Design" held in Linz in 1980; at this meeting, the entire history of design, its significance, and its many functions were discussed, including the role of the designer and the relationship between object and user. For the theory of design, this convention was extremely important.

Pluralism of style and influence, along with liberation from the suffocating philosophy of functionalism, now determined the course of design throughout Europe. In the process, the importance and

New Italian design in the Memphis style: Paolo Deganello's Documenta Chair, 1987 (made by Vitra). Deganello is considered an individualist who grew from the media spectacle surrounding design in the 1980s.

"About the phenomenon of design: Even the strictest theoreticians must see that with nothing more than logic, understanding, technical efficiency, and perfect aesthetics alone the needs of the socialized being man cannot be met."

Helmuth Gsöllpointner, Angela Hareiter, Laurids Ortner, "Forum Design," 1980

stature of design itself also grew. The 1980s became a decade of design. Design took over a key
role not only in marketing and advertising, but also
in the outfitting of the individual life-style, in
patterns of consumption and social modes of behavior. Design became a spectacle at exhibitions
and in the media. The new generation of designers
were no longer bound to certain companies, but
became marketing media stars in their own right.

New Design:
• Renunciation of ideological functionalism • Experimental works • Own production and distribution • Small series and unique pieces • Mixture
of styles • Unusual materials • Cosmopolitan feel
• Influences from subcultures • Irony, wit, and
provocativeness • Overstepping the boundaries
with art • Formation of groups of designers

The New Design
Memphis became the catalyst for a range of antifunctionalist developments in European design
gathered today under the rubric of "New Design."
In Spain, Germany, France, and Great Britain,
however, thoroughly independent forms and methods developed. Their thinking was independent of
industry and the partiality of functionalism, reflecting instead a metropolitan sense of life, the
changes in fashions, and the influences of subcultures and daily life in their designs, projects, and
statements. Also new was their method of using the
media as a platform for their work. Their works
were displayed in museum ex-
hibits
that drew

Shiro Kuramata, a major
exponent of minimalism in the
design of the 1980s. His wire-
netting chair, How High the
Moon, 1986–87 (made by
Vitra) is among his most
famous furniture pieces.

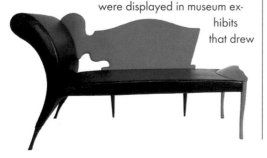

Chaise lounge, Prosim Sni
(Please Dream), by the Czech
star designer Borek Sipek,
chief representative of the
neo-Baroque direction in
New Design. Neo-Baroque
furniture quotes the involuted,
asymmetrical forms of the
Baroque, often using
luxuriously campy materials.

1968 – present

157

Groups in German New Design
- *Möbel perdu* (Lost Furniture)—Claudia Schneider-Esleben, Michel Feith—Hamburg, 1983
- *Pentagon*—Wolfgang Laubersheimer, Gerd Arens, Ralf Sommer, Reinhard Müller, Detlef Meyer-Voggenreiter—Cologne, 1985
- *Cocktail*—Renate von Brevern, Heike Mühlhaus—Berlin, 1981
- GIN̲BA̲NDE—Klaus-Achim Heine, Uwe Fischer—Frankfurt, 1985
- *Kunstflug* (Art Flight)—Heiko Bartels, Harald Hullmann, Hardy Fischer—Düsseldorf, 1982

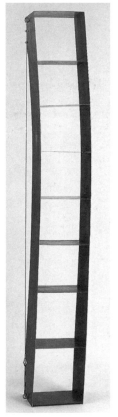

crowds of visitors that rivaled the usual crowds in traditional art shows.

New German Design

In Germany, where industry, design institutions, and academies had always stood firmly behind the power of "good form," the break with functionalism took on particular clarity. Since the end of the 1970s young academy graduates in the fields of architecture, art, and design had been engaged in experimental work in furniture and product design in various cities. Dissatisfied with "official" industrial design, education, and the working conditions in design departments and offices, they chose to create prototypes and individual pieces by hand. The aesthetics of these objects was based on collage and interruption. Unconventional materials—raw iron, plain steel or stone and concrete with wood, rubber, plush synthetics, or glass—were combined. Even half-finished items from building supply stores were reinterpreted from ready-made pieces into furniture. The intention behind the design of these objects was to shock and to question traditional design terms.

Wolfgang Laubersheimer's Tense Shelves (1984) is one of the most successful creations of New German Design.

In 1982 an exhibit was held in the Hamburg Museum for Art and Commerce where the new tendencies in design were coherently presented for the first time. Under the ironic title "Möbel perdu–Schöneres Wohnen" (Lost Furniture–More Beautiful Living), the exhibit presented the work of 39 designers and groups from five countries. Group exhibitions and experimental projects subsequently became important highlights for New Design everywhere.

Stiletto (Frank Schreiner), Consumer's Rest. The supermarket wagon redesigned into a chair, created as a prototype in 1983, was considered a provocative ready-made piece. Schreiner treated the customs of both daily life and consumption with irony. The chair has been in series production since 1990.

The principles of New German Design were varied, stretching from ironic splendor, the neo-Baroque with its penchant for kitsch, to the "Möbel perdu" of Claudia Schneider-Esleben, to minimalist designs and conceptual work by GINBANDE or Kunstflug. The language of the streets and the workday world emerged in the creations of Volker Albus and the provocative furniture of Siegfried Michael Syniuga and the ready-made objects by the Berlin Stiletto group. The somewhat more handcrafted work of the Berlin group Cocktail was inspired by ethnic patterns, while Andreas Brandolini ironically addressed petty bourgeois customs.

The climax of the movement was the 1986 exhibit "Gefühlscollagen–Wohnen von Sinnen" (Feeling-Collages–Living by the Senses) held in Düsseldorf. The project of the Design Workshop Berlin, initiated in 1988 by Christian Borngräber, introduced a return to industrial subjects in its attention to office furniture and the furnishing of public spaces such as train stations.

At the end of the 1980s, New Design in Germany was no longer as provocative as it was at first. It has been subjected to

Supported by idols: Artist Chair by Siegfried Michael Syniuga, 1987, square steel piping with cushion.

Ron Arad (1951–), Israeli sculptor, architect, and designer, first studied in Jerusalem, then with the Architectural Association in London. In 1981 he founded One Off Ltd. in London.

Jasper Morrison, Thinking Man's Chair, 1988, steel piping painted with antirust paint.

considerable criticism for its moderating trend. The idea of handling everything from design to distribution proved economically unfeasible. Even the road to the museum represented a dead-end for many designers. But through experimental work, the shock therapy of the new aesthetic and the experience gained from project work provided new impulses for furniture and industrial design. Many of the New Designers are active today as instructors at various academies.

England—the new simplicity

The forms and materials of English avant-garde design were similar in many respects to German New Design. Unlike Memphis and the elegant French designers, the "new" British designers preferred to work with rough materials, such as untreated steel or con-

Jörg Hundertpfund and Sylvia Rohbeck, File Kennel, and Bookrest, 1988, for the Design Workshop Berlin— new solutions for traditional office design work.

crete. They also distinguished themselves largely through a simplified language of material and form from other traditions in New Design that reveled in the neo-Baroque. The chief representatives of New Design in England were Ron Arad, Jasper Morrison, and Tom Dixon.

GINBANDE, pull-out table, Tabula Rasa, 1987 (Vitra). GINBANDE has worked since 1985 with conceptual design and raises questions about the meaning of function with experimental furniture. Tabula Rasa, for example, takes as its theme the social function of the table as a meeting place.

Jasper Morrison, New Items for the Home, Part I, installation for the Design Workshop Berlin, 1988. New simplicity in elementary forms and simple plywood furniture.

Jasper Morrison (1959–) studied design at the Kingston School of Art and Design in London. Since 1984 he has taught as a visiting instructor in Berlin, where he has close ties with the New German Design movement. In 1987 he took part in the "Documenta 8" exhibition, and since then has been included in many international shows. He produces designs for Vitra, Cappellini, Artemide, FSB, and Ritzenhoff.

In 1981 the Israeli architect and designer Ron Arad founded One Off Ltd. The studio's name refers to the programmatic production and distribution of individual pieces—unique specimens ("one-offs"). Arad experimented with different materials and also worked with ready-mades. His *Rover Chair*, made from the seat of a Land Rover, became famous, placing his London studio in the center of the New British Design.

Organically curvéd basket chair by Tom Dixon.

Jasper Morrison is perhaps the most important representative of New Design simplicity. He is known for his minimalistic plywood furniture with untreated surfaces. To protest the extravaance of the neo-Baroque and of frenzied media spectacles, he coined the term "no design."

Finally, Tom Dixon expounded a more expressive direction in New Design. Dixon experimented with iron, hardened rubber, and various basket weaves from which he created slim, organic forms.

Ron Arad, Well Tempered Chair, 1986–87, chrome steel sheet metal (Vitra).

1968 – present

Oscar Tusquets Blanca (1941–), architect and designer, was in the vanguard of the postmodern. He studied architecture in Barcelona and worked in the office of Alfonso Milá. In 1965 he was among the founders of the architect group Studio Per. In addition to numerous buildings in Barcelona, as a designer he has created jewelry, furniture, and consumer goods. Tusquets was one of the pioneers of the New Design in Spain.

New Design in Spain

Spain, and particularly Barcelona, plodded through the 1960s and 1970s under the influence of German "good form." In the 1980s, however, under the growing influence of Italy, Spain took its own creative step away from functionalism. The Catalonian capital city, which has always been a gathering place of artists and writers (it is the birthplace of Picasso), now became the site of a new beginning in Spanish design.

This development was favored by the entrance of Spain into the European Community, which connected Spanish industry with new markets and gave design an important role in export. Moreover, Barcelona was the host of the 1992 Summer Olympic Games.

Barcelona now developed a stylistic variety of New Design. Among the "new" Spanish designers we may count Tusquets Blanca, Clotet, Cortès, architect Arribas, and commercial artist Javier Mariscal, who was responsible for the controversial Olympic mascot.

Javier Mariscal, bar stool for the Duplex Bar in Valencia, Spain, 1980.

France—great stars in designer skies

At the beginning of the 1980s France was still influenced by Memphis, although the lively philosophical discussion of the postmodern was already influencing design at the end of the previous

Chairs by Oscar Tusquets (made by Driade). Overtones from art nouveau are unmistakable.

decade. In turning away from modernism, unusual combinations of color and material also character-ized New French Design, which first showed up in the furnishings of Paris's bars, cafés, stores, and restaurants, just as it had in other major European cities. In France, too, designers organized into groups such as "Nemo" and "Totem," but as a rule, it was always the design stars who stood for the avant-garde movement.

In fashion, the strongest branch of French de-sign, Jean-Paul Gaultier antagonized the public

Javier Mariscal (1950–) studied com-mercial art in Barcelona and has published his own comic books since 1972. At the end of the 1970s he started to design furniture, and in 1980 de-signed one of the first New Wave bars, the Duplex, in Valencia, followed by the more bar and restaurant furnishings. His comic charac-ter "Cobi" was the mascot of the 1992 Summer Olympic Games.

Javier Mariscal's comic figures from the Garriri Family are relatives of the Olympic mascot Cobi, and as pins have become recognizable symbols among Mariscal fans.

with materials taken from pornography—rubber, lacquer, and leather. With these, and even parts of the uniforms of concentration camp inmates, he broke both aesthetic and moral taboos. Though his name may not be a household word, his eccentric creations have been seen all over the world on Madonna, in her concerts and music videos.

In furniture and product design, the hottest new star was Philippe Starck. Starck stands as a crea-tive, independent thinker, though at the same time he has proved to be a skillful marketing strategist who ably uses himself to advertise his designs.

1968 – present

Representatives of New Design in France
Philippe Starck, Olivier Gagnère, Elizabeth Garouste, Mattia Bonetti, Jean-Paul Gaultier, Thierry Lecoute, Andrée Putman, Kristian Gavoille, André Dubreuil, Marie-Christine Dorner

Madonna in a dress by Jean-Paul Gaultier, 1990.

Philippe Starck (1949–) is probably the best-known representative of New Design in France. He was educated at the Ecole Nissim de Camondo in Paris. In 1968 he founded his first firm, specializing in inflatable objects, and became art director with Pierre Cardin in 1969. Since 1975 he has worked independently in interior and product design.

Philippe Starck, toothbrushes, 1989.

Unlike many representatives of New Design, Starck is not interested in protests or provocative single pieces, but designs salable and, in comparison to the other designers, relatively inexpensive products for mass production. He has not hesitated to borrow elements from past design styles—streamlined dynamic lines, organically formed handles, chair legs reminiscent of art nouveau, and more. His preference for unusual combinations of materials, such as plastic with aluminum, plush fabric with chrome, or glass with stone, is also characteristic of his design. His work ranges from spectacular interior design to daily consumer goods such as mineral water bottles and toothbrushes. In this respect, he may be compared with Raymond Loewy.

At the opposite pole from Starck we find Mattia Bonetti and Elizabeth Garouste. In contrast to Starck's smooth and rather cool designs, the works of Bonetti and Garouste are warm and at times wildly romantic. They stand as prominent representatives of the neo-Baroque, with a preference for materials such as satin, natural leather, and gilded bronze, which they work into luxury items.

The newest star of the French scene is the young designer Marie-Christine Dorner, who scored her first successes with a highly regarded interior design proposal for

1968 – present

Philippe Starck, Café Costes,
Paris, first floor, 1984. The
interior design of this café
along with its stools are world
famous.

a bar in Yokohama. As in the age of Art Deco,
New Design in France is distinguished from the
German and British varieties by its heightened
elegance.

After New Design

New Design at the beginning of the 1990s was
calm in comparison with the media excitement of
the early 1980s. Many of the once provocative
designs are now in museums, harmoniously juxta-
posed with classics of the modern period. There is
hardly an epoch that became a matter of history
so fast as the "wild eighties." Any number of designs that ten years earlier had been ridiculed as
old-fashioned hobby crafts or extravagant handwork are now produced in series by furniture companies or are being sold as cheap knock-offs in
large furniture markets. Like the punk movement,
and most antiestablishment waves, the protest ges-
tures of the New Design were absorbed by the
consumer goods industry and turned into fashion.

Many a critic prematurely predicted the failure
of the movement. Still, in addition to its influence
on the aesthetic sensibility of an entire generation—
which is no small matter—New Design has been

Philippe Starck's lemon press,
Juicy Salif, 1990, has meanwhile become an affordable
cult item.

1968 – present

165

Marie-Christine Dorner
(1960-).

responsible for important lines of thought in education and work in industrial design in the 1990s.

Coming into the nineties

Design and technology

The effects of technological advances are widespread. Not only has technology compelled us to rethink our understanding of design as a significant element in our social and cultural lives, but the lightning-paced technological development of recent years has changed the very function of many well-known components and consumer goods, creating new design tasks that must react to new areas and patterns of use. More than ever before, aesthetics has been influenced by technological development.

High tech

Once upon a time, the fascination of technology had been defeated by an increased preference for the aesthetic. Now the expression "high tech" has become a universally recognized stylistic term. High tech emphasizes the technological appearance of buildings through the demonstrative exterior positioning of plumbing pipes and elevator shafts, visible construction elements such as I-beams and steel traverses. Famous examples are the Pompidou Center (1977) by Renzo Piano and

Richard Rogers in Paris, the Hong Kong and Shanghai Bank (1981–85) by Norman Foster, and the Lloyds of London building (1986), also by Richard Rogers.

High-tech design brings together materials and prefabricated industrial pieces, for example,

Norman Foster, the Hong Kong and Shanghai Bank, Hong Kong, 1981–85.

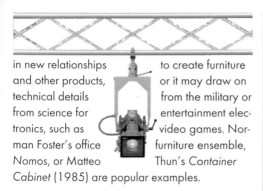

Roy Fleetwood, the Emanon 150 spotlight, 1990, manufactured by Erco, considered a leader in lighting technology. The electrical current is delivered through the latticed rails to which the lamp is fastened.

in new relationships and other products, technical details from science for electronics, such as Norman Foster's office furniture ensemble, Nomos, or Matteo Thun's *Container Cabinet* (1985) are popular examples. to create furniture or it may draw on from the military or entertainment electronics, such as video games.

Miniaturization

Far and away the most important technological development of recent years has come in the field of microelectronics. Many well-known devices have became ever smaller through advances in microchip technology, while the technology has spawned other equipment that was never before imaginable. The computer itself was once a huge machine occupying many rooms and weighing many tons. In the 1995 movie, *Apollo 13*, set in 1970, astronaut Jim Lovell explains to visiting dignitaries at NASA that one day they expect to have computers that fit in one room. While there are still large mainframe computers, their work capacity and speed are well beyond anything manageable in past decades, while what once required tons of machinery can now be performed on a small, sleek laptop.

For example: Sony

We have heard before about the limited space in the large cities of Japan, where apartments are extremely small. It is no accident that, for example, the stereo tower with components stacked on top of one another originated in Japan. It makes perfect sense that Japanese industry has pushed technical perfection in small appliances and equipment the furthest. The pioneer in this area was

Norman Foster, the Nomos office furniture system, a high-tech workplace complete with electric cable housings and various work surfaces from which the containers, the computer, and other equipment can be hung.

1968 – present

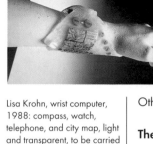

Lisa Krohn, wrist computer, 1988: compass, watch, telephone, and city map, light and transparent, to be carried on the wrist—the trend toward the dissolution of solid forms.

Sony, which by 1955 had built the first transistor radio, and had reduced it within three years to the size of an average shirt pocket. A year later, the first transistor television appeared and in 1966 Sony developed the first color video recorder for home use. Other technical advances have followed regularly.

The Walkman

In 1979 Sony CEO Akio Morita decided, despite resistance from his sales force, to manufacture a pocket-sized device to play audio cassettes: the Walkman. This device has had an unprecedented impact on the culture of the 1980s. With the Walkman, one can listen to music while riding the subway, jogging, or shopping. Today, the Walkman comes in many models, and although the name "Walkman" is a trademark of the Sony Corporation, the word has come to function generically, and is casually used to describe any small cassette player, regardless of the manufacturer. In 1988, Sony brought out the Watchman, a television counterpart of the Walkman; the portable CD player, the Discman, was based on the same principle, as is the Camcorder, a small, hand-held video recorder (1983), and the Data Discman, a portable CD-ROM player/reader.

Things disappear

The logical and sustained development of microelectronics has resulted in a virtual disappearance of "objects." It used to be simple enough to look at a manual typewriter and recognize its function, and then to look at an electric typewriter using a ball type element and deduce its function; the "word-processing" function of a computer disk is hardly apparent from its shape—though of course, the keyboard component of most word-processing systems has remained a constant. Still, even that is

The Walkman DC2 by Sony corresponds perfectly to the postmodern requirements of mobility, entertainment, and privacy.

Automated ticket and service kiosk by the Düsseldorf group Kunstflug, 1987. With the corresponding software, this kiosk can sell tickets, make complete travel arrangements, reserve seats, sell theater tickets and city maps, and dispense official forms. In order to make the wide range of services clear and accessible to the user, only one function and command line is visible on the screen at a time. For users who feel unsure of themselves, an operator is available to give the necessary help by video.

subject to change, as more users prefer trackballs and mice. In any event, it is impossible to differentiate one functional application of computer software from another based solely on the form of the disk on which it is contained, or even of the hardware in which it is used. To convey differences among functions, the designer in the electronic age has a range of new tasks, including the design of surfaces, which was once scorned as a matter of mere styling. Design concerns not only the appearance of tangible forms, but also to intangible processes and information.

Computers and design

Since the 1980s, designing has not only been done for computers but by them as well. CAD/ CAM (computer-assisted design/computer-assisted manufacturing) became the buzz words for new possibilities in planning and production, especially for so-called high-tech products. New graphic programs have made it possible to simulate a product on the screen, and not only to design it, but also to modify important technical and ecological data. The advantage of the computerized process lies in the graphic vividness of the representation and the concomitant flexibility of the design process.

Functions into symbols: RIA, the automated travel information service of the German Railroad has offered simple user-friendly travel schedules in several languages since 1994. The screen lies like an open book in front of the prospective traveler.

1968 – present

169

Designs by computer: ergonomic study with the help of
computerized visualization by
Mercedes Benz (above), and
frogdesign, an electronic design study for Yamaha model
Frog 750, 1985 (below).

Design and marketing

The design boom of the 1980s clearly underlined the role of design in corporate politics. By the beginning of the 1980s most consumer goods were already technically mature; within a price class, for the most part, one product was as well made as another. Under such circumstances, the only mechanism left for a company to use to compete in the marketplace is to distinguish its products by means of their design.

In more and more businesses design became a natural component of corporate identity: products assumed the images of the corporation as well as for the consumer. Many firms, however, never developed any particular design policy or line, but took a shortcut by designating anything that was more colorful or in some way out of the ordinary a "designer piece." As a marketing ploy, they might tack on a designer's name (for the more ruthless and desperate manufacturer, the designer might well be fictional). A given line might be described as a "limited edition" as an incentive for con-sumers to buy right away. To appeal to the seem-ingly infinite worlds of public taste, manufacturers sought to add individualized patterns, exteriors, surfaces, and details to products that otherwise were technically identical.

For example: The Swatch

In 1983 the world of watches was turned upside down by a process that has come to be known as "Swatchification." The company responsible, Swatch, was established as a joint venture by sev-eral large Swiss watchmakers in Biel, Switzerland.

Swatch watches are inexpensive, nonreparable wristwatches that consciously incorporate into their design the transitory nature of fashion, the *Zeitgeist*, and life-styles, and offer different looks by variation in details. The original collection of Swatches was content to offer single-color straps and four style directions: classic, high-tech, fashion, and sport. Since then, however, the palette of watch straps and faces has grown almost beyond grasp. The watches are either created by famous designers like Matteo Thun and Alessandro Mendini, or use motifs of famous artists such as Keith Haring and Mimmo Paladino. Swatch became a model of the use of individualized design as a market strategy in the 1980s.

Design management and service design

The importance of design as a strategic management tool is reflected in the newly coined term "design management." Planning a product increasingly includes organizational, economic, legal, and marketing questions in addition to the question of form.

The field of design is expanding, and today the concept of corporate design also involves television advertising, telephone marketing, and software. At the same time, unity of image is not a goal sought at any price; individualization also plays a role in a company's cultivation of its image. Many independent design offices offer a complete service that stretches beyond the product itself to the design of the organizational structure and of manners within the company.

Design and culture

The relation of New Design to art; the interdisciplinary connections between the applied arts, art,

Individualization: The watch, formerly a once-in-a-lifetime purchase, or even an heirloom, is transformed into a changeable fashion accessory. Every year, Swatch brings out two new collections covering a broad panorama of tastes. Here, Flumotions from the Fall/Winter 1987 collection (*left*) and African-Can from Spring/Summer 1990.

and industry; the numerous museum exhibitions; the rise of the star designer—all these aspects of design have created a consciousness of design as a justified part of culture among the general public. Design museums and departments in art museums have sprouted up around the world. At the "Documenta 8" exhibition—possibly the most important art exhibit in the world—design first occupied a section of its own in 1987. Retrospectives, a flood of publications, and cheerful revivals of the artifacts of past eras made the decade of the 1980s into a virtual "crash course" in the history of design.

As with music, theater, art films, and art, design has become dependent on sponsorship or underwriting by businesses that choose cultural sponsorship as a part of their corporate identity. Even furniture companies such as the Swiss manufacturer Vitra will issue an edition of individual pieces or limited editions. The tobacco company Philip Morris offers a prize for young designers and uses the popularity and cultural recognition of design to enhance its own image—something it sorely needs in an era when the public image of smoking and tobacco products is not terribly positive, and the reputation of the firm is decaying by the minute.

For example: Vitra

The Swiss furniture maker Vitra, in Weil on Rhine, has made the cultural understanding of design an

The Design Museum in Butler's Wharf Dockland was established in 1989 with the support of the Terence Conran Foundation.

The Vitra Design Museum in Weil on Rhine, Switzerland, designed by architect Frank O. Gehry, 1989. Design has become an indispensable component of Vitra's corporate identity. In addition to a collection of classics, Vitra will issue an edition, giving a platform to avant-garde designs as single pieces or small series. The Design Museum displays a cross-section of the history of furniture design and houses one of the largest design collections in the world today. Vitra expanded its grounds in 1991 with a factory fire department building designed by Iraqi architect Zaha M. Hadid, and in 1993 with a conference pavilion designed by Tadao Ando. The company's design, architecture, and aesthetic appearance constitute its "corporate identity," which bears comparison with the corporate culture created by Peter Behrens for the German company, AEG.

essential component of its corporate policy. Established in 1934 by W. Fehlbaum, Vitra has placed particular value on design since 1957–58 when it began the licensed production of furniture by designers Charles Eames and George Nelson. Today Vitra produces office and commercial furniture for both the public and the private sector. Its products are developed in collaboration with important designers such as Mario Bellini, Antonio Citterio, Jasper Morrison, Philippe Starck, and others. The present owner, R. Fehlbaum, erected a museum, planned by the American architect Frank O. Gehry, in 1989 to house a design collection that has subsequently been assembled. In 1995 Vitra received the European Design Prize for its exemplary total appearance, with its comprehensive concept of architecture and design.

Design and the environment

The expanded vision of design today cannot overlook environmental issues. A "good" product today spares resources and the environment. Consumers are increasingly sensitive to environmental issues and are less likely to support products known to represent ecological dangers. Mountains of chlorine-bleached paper, toxic markers, and other hazardous office waste demand that designers assume responsibility for the materials and production processes used in their designs. Design-

1968 – present

The bag Umbra (1994) by Katja Horst (Reisenthel, Puchheim, Germany) consists of small, pressed scraps of leather, rubber, and natural oils and fats. The surface has a pattern stamped on it. The aesthetics of the eco-design has come a long way from the standards of counter-culture.

Factor Design, ad for recycled paper by the Paper Factory in Gmund. Both the paper and the ad received the "Design Plus" prize in 1994.

ers, for their part, have always resisted being seen as either capitalist stooges or mere "marketing decorators." It is in their interest, for love or for money, to demonstrate their social concern and environmental awareness.

It is no longer sufficient, for "ecological" design, simply to express a preference for jute instead of plastic—that is, for natural versus synthetic materials. To be ecological, a product, even a high-tech product, must be durable and recyclable, as well as having some intrinsic aesthetic appeal. New ideas along these lines are manifold—ranging from edible packaging made of starch or waffles (many companies in the United States actually use real popcorn instead of polystyrene "popcorn" for shipping and packaging), to completely recyclable computers made without any superfluous composite materials.

It does not really matter if some "eco-products" are used merely to enhance a company's image. The fact is that ecological products and ecological manufacturing are necessary, and if a company sees the perception of environmental concern as a positive part of its image—even if it is actually motivated by economic concerns stemming from rising waste removal costs and government mandates to increase recycling programs—this helps promote wider awareness of environmental issues, and make a difference.

Design and sense

Consumers, like manufacturers and designers, are also changing. Many buyers are no longer looking for the shrill and the showy, but look instead, over and above a product's practical value, for its individuality, authenticity, and meaning for their lives. Years of argument and provocation have made certain classic designs and archetypes seem safe and reliable, and it is to these designs that many consumers still turn.

What's ahead?

Over the many years of its history, design has changed, stretched, and expanded in its definition and range of responsibilities. There is far more to design today than deciding what something will look like. Even if one prefers not to inflate the stature of design, it is impossible to deny the omnipresent role of design in industry and in daily life—and it is wise not to deny its subtle power as well. The importance of design will continue to grow as its field of responsibilities increases. In spite of the often lamented fragmentation of the market, the variety of products and forms will probably continue to expand, because the struggle for product individuality and the differences among competitors in contracting markets will naturally provoke such development.

It is not easy to take stock of the present condition of design. Theoreticians and critics as well as the creators of design are devoting themselves more and more, as in the established arts of painting and architecture, to special areas and individual problems. The future remains a question.

A change in consciousness: a bathroom by Philippe Starck, 1994 (for Axor, Duravit, and Hoesch), uses as a frame of reference simple archtypical shapes such as washtubs, pumps, and pails, and brings the most modern sanitation fixtures into a functional and modestly harmonious ambience. Mottos such as "New Simplicity" or "Back to Basics" indicate—in addition to common sense for the consumer and market success for the manufacturer—the first signs of a kind of return to rationality.

1968 – present

175

Glossary

Antifunctionalism: Reaction against the one-sided dominance of functionalism. Especially since the late 1950s, many designers and theoreticians have turned away from the overly narrow and moralistic principles of a design philosophy that measures everything according to the purely technical function of an object.

Briefing: Information, provided to the designers by the manufacturer, containing all the important requirements for a product, such as color, material, product description, scheduling, etc.

CAD/CAM (computer-aided design/computer-aided manufacture): Computer-supported design and/or production, utilized particularly in technical production.

Commercial art: Production of artistically designed consumer commodities; concept often denigrated by both artists (because the products lack the autonomy and innovativeness of pure artistic creation) and by industrial designers (because the products usually involve hand labor); the term therefore is often employed polemically to disqualify design proposals.

Consultant designer: Freelance design consultant employed by corporations and institutions.

Corporate design: An aspect of corporate identity that relies on a unified principle of design for the products as well as a company's overall public image.

Corporate identity: The personality, philosophy, and/or identity of a firm.

Corporate image: The impression a company makes on the public.

documenta: Since 1955, an important exhibition of contemporary international art held in Kassel, Germany.

Eclecticism (from Greek *eklegein* = to choose): A derogatory reference for art that arbitrarily mixes stylistic elements from various historical periods without making creative contributions of its own.

Eco-design: Design that includes ecological aspects in product planning.

Ergonomics: Study of the relation between the worker and working conditions—central in particular to the design of office furniture since the 1960s.

Functionalism: In architecture and design, the stylistic concept that raises the technical function of an object to the sole criterion of form and rejects decoration and coloration; usually seen as arising from Sullivan's statement, "Form follows function."

High tech: Since the late 1970s and 1980s, a style that elevates technology to an aesthetic principle in architecture and design; the style is characterized by visible structural elements such as pipes, cables, and supports, and by materials such as steel, sheet metal, and glass, even in the home.

Intrinsic value: The value of a product measured according to its ability to fulfill its purpose, that is, according to its practical as well as its aesthetic or symbolic function; often interpreted in a narrow sense.

Kitsch: A derogatory reference to tasteless objects whose exaggerated aesthetics dishonestly and sentimentally appeals to the feelings; the term probably arose from the German *verkitschen*, a practice of selling cheap paintings to tourists in Munich in the 1880s.

Limited series: A product or designer object, especially furniture, made in small quantities, often by hand; since the 1980s, also found increasingly in industrial design with the help of computer-guided machines.

Logo: An easily recognized emblem of a firm or a brand.

Neo-Baroque: Stylistic tendency of the New Design of the 1980s and 1990s relying on richly decorated, often ironically kitschy, designs; term derived from the employment of Baroque elements of the second half of the 19th century.

Pop art: An artistic movement of the 1960s employing the products of mass culture and subculture (such as comics, advertising, magazines, and films) ironically or exaltingly as a theme; movement had a strong influence on design.

Postmodern: Since the 1970s, the attempt in art, architecture, and design to overcome progress-oriented modernism and calcified functionalism through (sometimes) ironically historical stylistic citations and unusual combinations of form and color; hotly debated, and at times employed polemically, since the late 1970s and 1980s.

Prototype: The first model of a new product, trying out the materials, form, and function for later serial production.

Ready-made: A daily commodity taken out of its original context and made into a work of art; the "father of the ready-made" is Marcel Duchamp; in design, the process was used especially in the 1980s for experimental work.

Recycling design: Design involving the reuse of materials such as plastic, metal, paper, leather, etc.

Redesign: Reworking of an already existing product in order to improve it formally or functionally; term used ironically by Alchimia designers in their criticism of past styles or objects from design history.

Re-edition: Reproduction of a well-known product (design) that has been out of production for an extended period, or existed only as a design proposal; especially design classics like Bauhaus chairs or other objects of early modernism have been reproduced since the end of the 1960s.

Style: A typical form for a time period or region.

Total work of art: Ideal synthesis of various arts into a single impression, seen for example in art nouveau and Bauhaus.

Unique piece: Individually produced piece, usually made by hand; in New Design, often designates a form of ground-breaking experimental work.

A chronological history of design

1765	James Watt develops the steam engine
1774	The first Shaker community is founded in the United States
1835	Samuel Colt invents the revolver
1844	Samuel Morse sends the first telegram
1847–48	Marx and Engels, *Communist Manifesto*
1851	Crystal Palace is designed by J. Paxton for the Great Exhibition in London
1854	Thonet presents the first bentwood chairs
1859	Thonet introduces Chair No. 14
1869	The magazine *Die Jugend* (Youth) begins publication
1870	The era of German industrial expansion begins
1873	Industrial production of Remington typewriters begins
1875	Thomas Edison invents the incandescent light bulb
1876	Alexander Graham Bell demonstrates the telephone at the World's Fair in Philadelphia
1889	The Eiffel Tower is built for the Paris Exposition
1893	The Chicago World's Fair; Victor Horta designs the Tassel House in Brussels
1897	Vienna Secession
1898	The Dresden Workshops for Commercial Art are established
1899	Louis Henry Sullivan designs the Carson, Pirie and Scott Department Store, Chicago
1900	Hector Guimard designs entrances to the Paris Metro
1904	First garden city in England

A chronological history of design

1904–06 Otto Wagner designs the Postal Savings Bank in Vienna

1905 Josef Hoffman designs the Stoclet Palace in Brussels

1907 Leo Henry Baekeland invents Bakelite; the German Work Union (Werkbund) is established; Peter Behrens begins working with AEG

1908 Ford introduces the Model T car; Adolf Loos, *Ornament and Crime*

1909 Filippo Tommaso Marinetti issues the *First Futurist Manifesto*

1913 The first assembly line starts up at the Ford Motor Company; the Woolworth Building is built in New York; *Fagus Works* by Walter Gropius

1914 International Werkbund Exhibition in Cologne; Werkbund dispute

1917 Foundation of De Stijl group; Gerrit Rietveld designs the Red and Blue Chair

1919 Raymond Loewy moves from Paris to New York; Founding Manifesto of the Bauhaus

1920 Vladimir Tatlin: Monument for the Third International

1921 Coco Chanel markets Chanel No. 5

1923 László Moholy-Nagy at the Bauhaus; Le Corbusier, *Towards a New Architecture*

1924 Gerrit Rietveld builds Schröder House in Utrecht; Wagenfeld Lamp (Bauhaus)

1925 The Werkbund newspaper *Die Form* begins publication; Marcel Breuer designs the Wassily Chair; The Exposition Internationale des Arts Décoratifs et Industriels Modernes is held in Paris; the Bauhaus moves to Dessau

1926 Adolf Loos designs Tzara House in Paris; J.J.P. Oud designs the Café de Unie in Rotterdam

1927 Werkbund Exhibition, "The Apartment"; the Weissenhof Settlement is established in Stuttgart

1928 Gió Ponti founds the magazine *Domus*; Le Corbusier, P. Jeaneret, C. Perriand, Chairs LC3 and LC4

1928–29 Hannes Meyer is named director of the Bauhaus

1929 Mies van der Rohe designs the German Pavilion and Barcelona Chair, exhibits at the World's Fair in Barcelona; Raymond Loewy designs the Gestetner Duplicator; the Great Depression; founding of the Museum of Modern Art in New York City

1930 Werkbund Exhibition, Paris; the Chrysler Building, New York; Eckart Muthesius does the interior design for the Palace at Indore; Mies van der Rohe becomes the last director of the Bauhaus

1932 Aerodynamic locomotives by Bel Geddes, Dreyfuss, and Loewy; founding of the Cranbrook Academy; the Empire State Building, New York

1933 Nazis seize power in Germany; support for the spread of radio; the Bauhaus is closed

1934 Gerrit Rietveld, Zig-Zag Chair; F. Porsche designs prototypes of the Volkswagen

1935 Pierre-Jules Boulanger and André Lefèbvre design a prototype of the Citroen 2CV

1935–39 Alvar Aalto, Chair 406 (Suspended Chair of Plywood)

1937 Walter Gropius teaches at the Harvard School of Architecture; Wallace Hume Carothers patents nylon;

A chronological history of design

World Exhibition in Paris; László Moholy-Nagy founds the New Bauhaus in Chicago

1938 Mies van der Rohe becomes head of the Illinois Institute of Technology in Chicago; founding of the Volkswagen factory in Wolfsburg, Germany; Raymond Loewy designs the Locomotive S1 for the Pennsylvania Railroad

1939 World's Fair in New York, "Building the World of Tomorrow"

1940 Charles Eames and Eero Saarinen win the contest "Organic Design in Home Furnishing" of the Museum of Modern Art, New York; Raymond Loewy designs the Lucky Strike package

1946 First model of the legendary Vespa motor scooter

1947 The German Werkbund reestablished

1949 Werkbund exhibit "New Living" is held in Cologne

1951 First color televisions sold in the United States; founding of the Council for Design in Darmstadt

1952 Arne Jacobsen, Ameise Chair; invention of polypropylene

1953 Beginning of instruction at the Academy for Design in Ulm

1954 First awarding of the Compasso d'Oro prize, established by the department store La Rinascente; the Ulm Stool is designed by M. Bill and H. Gugelot

1956–59 Frank Lloyd Wright designs the Guggenheim Museum in New York

1958 World's Fair in Brussels; Charles Eames, Lounge Chair

1959 Founding of the VDID (Union of German Industrial Designers)

1965 Marco Zanuso designs the folding radio, TS 502, for Brionvega; Theodor W. Adorno, *Functionalism Today*; miniskirts become fashionable

1966 Founding of the Superstudio in Milan

1968 Closing of the Academy for Design in Ulm; Panton, Side Chair; Werner Nehls, *The Sacred Cows of Functionalism Must Be Sacrificed*

1969 Ettore Sottsass designs the portable typewriter Valentine for Olivetti; Joe Colombo presents the Central Living Block at the Visiona

Exhibit in Cologne; man first walks on the moon; Giancarlo Piretti designs the Plia folding chair

1970 International Design Center, Berlin; Verner Panton presents Landscapes for Living at the Visiona Exhibit at the Cologne Furniture Fair

1972 The exhibition, "Italy. The New Domestic Landscape," opens at the Museum of Modern Art in New York; Richard Sapper designs the Tizio lamp

1973 Mario Bellini designs the adding machine Divisumma 18 for Olivetti; oil crisis; "Global Tools" exhibit in Milan

1974 The Tire Sofa by Des-in studio; Roland Moreno develops the first memory card for computer data

1975 Charles Jencks popularizes the term "postmodern;" opening of IKEA

1976 Founding of Studio Alchimia

1977 Documenta 6 in Kassel, Germany, presents Utopian Design; opening of the Georges Pompidou Center in Paris

1978–82 Philip Johnson designs the AT&T

A chronological history of design ... Museums

Building in New York

1979 Sony introduces the Walkman; Philips and Sony develop the CD; IBM manufactures the first laser printer

1980 Alessi designs household commodities together with contemporary architects; founding of the Memphis studio; Apple Corp. introduces the Macintosh computer; "Forum Design" in Linz

1981 Ettore Sottsass, Carlton

1982 The exhibition "Lost Furniture—More Beautiful Living" (Möbel perdu) is held in the Hamburg Museum for Art and Trade; J.-F. Lyotard, *Postmodern Science*

1983 Founding of Swatch; founding of Möbel perdu in Hamburg

1985 Founding of Pentagon

1986 Exhibition "Living from the Senses" held in Düsseldorf; R. Rogers designs the Lloyds Building in London; Ron Arad designs the Well-Tempered Chair

1987 The New Design studio has its own section at documenta in Kassel

1988 Design Workshop, Berlin

1989 Design Museum, London; Design Museum of the Vitra Company in Weil on Rhine, Switzerland

1990 Philippe Starck designs Floucaril toothbrush

1991 N. Foster designs the Olympia television tower in Barcelona

1992 World's Fair Expo, Seville

1993 The exhibit "Design, Mirror of an Age" is held in the Grand Palace in Paris

Museums and design collections

Amsterdam
Stedelijk Museum of Modern Art
Paulus Potterstraat 13
Postbus 5082
NL–1070 AB Amsterdam

Basel
Museum für Gestaltung Basel
Spalenvorstadt 2
CH–4003 Basel

Berlin
Bauhaus-Archiv
Museum für Gestaltung
Klingelhöferstraße 14
D–10785 Berlin

Kunstgewerbemuseum Berlin
Matthäikirchplatz
D–10785 Berlin

Werbund-Archiv,
Museum der Alltagskultur des 20. Jahrhunderts
Martin-Gropius-Bau
Stresemannstraße 110
D–10963 Berlin

Cambridge, MA
The MIT Museum
265 Massachusetts Ave.
Cambridge, MA 02139

Chicago
The Art Institute of Chicago
Michigan Ave.
Chicago, IL 60603

Cologne
Museum für Angewandte Kunst
An der Rechtschule
D–50667 Cologne

Copenhagen
Kunstindustrimuseet
Bredgade 68
DK–1260 Copenhagen

Dessau
Bauhaus
Gropiusallee 38
D–06846 Dessau

Frankenberg
Thonet-Museum
Michael-Thonet-Straße 1
D–35066 Frankenberg

Frankfurt/Main
Museum für Kunsthandwerk
(Designsammlung im Aufbau)
Schaumainkai 17
D–60594 Frankfurt/Main

Museums and Design Collections ... Bibliography

Glasgow
Hunterian Art Gallery
University of Glasgow
Glasgow G12 8QQ
UK

Hamburg
Museum für Kunst u.
Gewerbe
Steintorplatz 1
D-20099 Hamburg

Helsinki
Museum of Applied Arts
(Taideteollisuusmuseo)
Korkeavuorenkatu 23
SF-00130 Helsinki

London
Design Museum
Butler's Wharf
Shad Thames
London SE1 2YD

Victoria and Albert Museum
Cromwell Road, South
Kensington
London SW7 2RL

Milan
Museo Alchimia
Via Torino 668
I-20123 Milan

Munich
Die Neue Sammlung
Prinzregentenstraße 3
D-80538 Munich

New York
Cooper-Hewitt Museum
Smithsonian Institution
National Museum of Design
2 East 91 Street
New York, NY 10128

Museum of Modern Art
11 West 53rd Street,
New York, NY 10019

New York Design Center
Thompson Ave.
Long Island City
New York, NY 11101

Oslo
Kunstindustrimuseet i Oslo
Olavsgate 1
N-0165 Oslo

Paris
Centre Georges Pompidou
Centre de Création
Industrielle
31 Rue Saint Merri
F-75191 Paris

Musée des Arts Décoratifs
107 rue de Rivoli
F-75001 Paris

Musée d'Orsay
62 rue de Lille
F-75007 Paris

Stockholm
Nationalmuseum
S. Blasieholmshamnen
Box 1 61 76
S-10324 Stockholm

Trondheim
Nordenfjeldske
Kunstindustrimuseet
Munkegaten 5
N-7000 Trondheim

Vienna
Österreichisches Museum
für Angewandte Kunst
Stubenring 5
A-1010 Vienna

Weil am Rhein
Vitra Design Museum
Charles-Eames-Straße 1
D-79576 Weil am Rhein

Zürich
Museum für Gestaltung
Zürich
Ausstellungsstrasse 60
CH-8005 Zürich

Centre Le Corbusier
Heidi-Weber-Haus
Höschgasse 8
CH-8008 Zürich

Bibliography

Aitken, John, & George Mills. Design & Technology. New York: State Mutual Book & Periodical Service, Ltd., 1989.

Aldersey-Williams, Hugh. World Design: Nationalism & Globalism in Design. New York: Rizzoli International Publications, Inc., 1992.

Anikst, Mikhail, ed. Soviet Commercial Design of the Twenties. New York: Abbeville Press, Inc., 1991.

Anscombe, Isabelle. A Woman's Touch: Women in Design from 1860 to the Present Day. New York: Viking Penguin, 1984.

Art and Design (AD Publications, London).

Assemblage (MIT Press, Cambridge, MA).

Baker, Robin. Designing the Future. New York: Thames & Hudson, 1993.

Baker, Eric. Great Inventions, Good Intentions: An Illus-

trated History of American Design Patents. San Francisco: Chronicle Books, 1990.

Bangert, Albrecht. *Eighties Style: Designs of the Decade.* New York: Abbeville Press, Inc., 1990.

Bauhaus: A History 1919–1933. Leverett: Rector Press, Ltd., 1994.

Beer, Eileene H. *Scandinavian Design: Objects of a Life Style.* Minneapolis: American-Scandinavian Foundation, 1975.

Berkom, Bev Ulsrud van. *Ancient Scandinavian Designs.* Owings Mills: Stemmer House Publications, Inc., 1985.

Best-Maugard, Adolfo. *Method for Creative Design.* New York: Dover Publications, Inc., 1990.

Bevlin, Marjorie. *Design Through Discovery.* 6th ed. Orlando: Harcourt Brace College Publishers, 1993.

Bicknell, J. & McQuiston, L., eds. *Design for Need.* Elkins Park: Franklin Book Co., Inc., 1977.

Bierut, Michael, et al, eds. *Looking Closer: Critical Writings on Graphic Design.* New York: Allworth Press, 1994.

Blaich, Robert, & Janet Blaich. *Product Design & Corporate Strategy: Managing the Connection for Competitive Advantage.* New York: The McGraw-Hill Companies, 1993. *Blueprint* (London).

Bothwell, Dorr, & Marlys Mayfield. *Notan: The Dark-Light Principle of Design.* Reprint ed. New York: Dover Publications, Inc.

Bowe, Nicola G., ed. *The Search for Vernacular Expression in Turn-of-the-Century Design.* Portland: International Specialized Book Services, 1993.

Boym, Constantin. *New Russian Design.* New York: Rizzoli International Publications, Inc., 1992.

Branzi, Andrea. *The Hot House: Italian New Wave Design.* Translated by C.H. Evans. Cambridge: MIT Press, 1984.

Bridgewater, Gill, & Allan Bridgewater. *Traditional & Folk Designs.* Woodstock: Arthur L. Schwartz & Co., Inc., 1990.

Brommer, Gerald F. *Movement & Rhythm: Principles of Design.* (Concepts of Design Ser.) Woodstock: Arthur Schwartz & Co., Inc., 1975.

Bucciarelli, Louis L. *Designing Engineers.* (Inside Windows Guides Ser.) Cambridge: MIT Press, 1994.

Buchanan, Richard, & Victor Margolin, eds. *Discovering Design: Explorations in Design Studies.* Chicago: University of Chicago Press, 1995.

Burckhart, Lucius. *The Werkbund.* New York: State Mutual Book & Periodical Service, Ltd., 1987.

Busche, Don, & Bernice Glenn. *The Desktop Design Workbook.* Englewood Cliffs: Prentice Hall, 1992.

Byars, Mel. *The Design Encyclopedia.* New York: John Wiley & Sons, Inc., 1994.

Calloway, Stephen, ed. *Liberty of London: Masters of Style & Decoration.* New York: Little, Brown & Co., 1992.

Carbarga, Leslie. *Trademark Designs of the Twenties.* New York: Dover Publications, Inc., 1991.

Carter, David E., ed. *Evolution of Design.* New York: Art Direction Book Co., 1985.

Chermayeff, Ivan. *Growing by Design.* New York: Van Nostrand Reinhold, 1991.

Clemenshaw, Doug. *Design in Plastics.* Blount & Co. Staff, ed. Rockport: Rockport Publishers, 1989.

Collins, Michael. *Post-Modern Design.* London: Academy Editions, 1989.

Conway, Hazel, ed. *Design History: A Student's Handbook.* New York: Routledge, Chapman & Hall, Inc., 1987.

Cooke, Catherine. *Beyond Zero: The Russian Avant-Garde, 1915–1932 Art, Architecture, & Design.* New York: Solomon R. Guggenheim Museum, 1992.

Cooper, Wendy A. *Classical Taste in America, 1800–1840.* New York: Abbeville Press, Inc., 1993.

Cooper-Hewitt, National Museum of Design, Smithsonian Institution Staff. *The Edge of the Millennium.* Velavich, Susan, ed. New York: Watson-Guptill Publications, Inc., 1993.

Cross, Nigel, ed. *Developments in Design Methodology.* Reprint ed. Ann Arbor: Books on Demand.

Bibliography

Crozier, Ray. *Manufactured Pleasures: Psychological Responses to Design.* New York: St. Martin's Press, Inc., 1994.

Dale, Rodney, & Henry Dale. *The Industrial Revolution.* Reprinted ed. New York: Oxford University Press, Inc., 1994.

De Noblet, Jocelyn, ed. *Industrial Design: Reflection of a Century.* New York: Abbeville Press, Inc.

DeSiano. *Principles & Elements of Art & Design.* Unionville: Trillium Press, 1992.

Design: Tradition & Change. Reprint ed. Columbia: South Asia books, 1986.

Design (Design Council, London).

Design Arts (Cooper Union, New York).

Design Council Staff. *Information Technology & the Leisure Industry: The Textiles Industry & the Car Industry.* New York: State Mutual Book & Periodical Service, Ltd., 1987.

Royal Designers on Design. New York: State Mutual Book & Periodical Service, Ltd., 1987.

Design Issues (University of Illinois).

Design Management Journal (Boston).

Design on File. New York: Facts on File.

Design Quarterly (Walker Art Center, Minneapolis).

Design Studies (IPC Science and Technology Press, Guildford, UK).

Doordan, Denis, ed. *Design History: An Anthology.* Cambridge: MIT Press, 1995.

Dormer, Peter. *The Meaning of Modern Design: Towards the Twenty-First Century.* New York: Thames & Hudson, 1990.

Dormer, Peter. *Design since Nineteen Forty-Five.* New York: Thames & Hudson, 1993.

Drwal, Frances. *Polish Wycinanki Designs.* Owings Mills: Stemmer House Publications, Inc., 1984.

Express (Metropolis Enterprises, New York).

Falk, Peter H. *Annual Exhibition Record of the National Academy of Design: 1901–1950.* Madison, CT: Sound View Press, 1990.

Ferebee, Ann. *A History of Design from the Victorian Era to the Present.* Blue Ridge Summit: TAB Books, 1992.

Forty, Adrian. *Objects of Desire: Design and Society 1750–1980.* New York: Thames & Hudson, 1992.

Freeman, John C., & Nancy Ruhling. *The Illustrated Encyclopedia of Victoriana: A Comprehensive Guide to the Designs, Customs, & Inventions of the Victorian Era.* Philadelphia: Running Press Book Publishers, 1994.

Friedman, Dan. *Dan Friedman: Radical Modernism.* New Haven: Yale University Press, 1994.

Gere, Charlotte, & Michael Whiteway. *Nineteenth Century Design.* New York: Harry N. Abrams, Inc., 1994.

Gabra-Liddell, Meret, ed. *Alessi: The Design Factory.*

New York: St. Martin's Press, 1994.

Garner, Philippe. *The Contemporary Decorative Arts from 1940 to the Present Day.* Oxford: Phaidon, 1980.

Gilbert, Anne. *Sixties' & Seventies' Designs & Memorabilia: Identification & Price Guide.* New York: Avon Books.

—. *Forties' & Fifties' Designs & Memorabilia: Identification & Price Guide.* New York: Avon Books.

Heller, Steven, & Anne Fink. *Low-Budget, High-Quality Design.* New York: Watson-Guptill Publications, Inc., 1990.

Heller, Steven, & Julie Lasky. *Borrowed Design: Use & Abuse of Historical Form.* New York: Van Nostrand Reinhold, 1993.

Hiesinger, Kathryn, & George Marcus. *Landmarks of Twentieth-Century Design.* New York: Abbeville Press, Inc., 1993.

Hietala, Thomas R. *Manifest Design: Anxious Aggrandizement in Late Jacksonian America.* reprint ed. Ithaca: Cornell University Press, 1990

Holdridge, Barbara. *Aubrey Beardsley Designs from the Age of Chivalry.* Owings Mills: Stemmer House Publishers, Inc., 1983.

Hornung, Clarence P. *Treasury of American Design & Antiques.* Avenal: Random House Value Publishing, Inc., 1989.

International Design Yearbook (Abbeville Press).

Bibliography

Jackson, Holbrook. *William Morris and the Arts & Crafts.* New York: Gordon Press Publishers, 1972.

Jackson, Lesley. *The New Look: Design in the Fifties.* New York: Thames & Hudson, 1991.

Journal of Design History (Oxford, UK).

Julier, Guy. *The Thames & Hudson Encyclopedia of Twentieth Century Design & Designers.* New York: Thames & Hudson, 1993.

Kasprisin, R. *Visual Thinking for Architecture & Design.* New York: Van Nostrand Reinhold, 1994.

Lauer, David A. *Design Basics.* 3rd ed. Orlando: Harcourt Brace College Publishers, 1990.

Lawson, B. *How Designers Think.* 2nd ed. Newton: Butterworth-Heinemann, 1990.

Leonard, R.C., & C.A. Glassgold, eds. *Modern American Design, by the American Union of Decorative Artists and Craftsmen.* New York: Acanthus Press, 1992.

Lewalski, Zdzislaw M. *Product Esthetics: An Interpretation for Designers.* Carson City: Design Development Engineering Press, 1988.

Mahoney, Jean, & Peggy L. Rao. *At Home with Japanese Design: Accents, Structure & Spirit.* Boston: Charles E. Tuttle Co., Inc., 1990.

Margolin, Victor, intro. *Design Discourse: History, Theory, Criticism.* Chicago: University of Chicago Press, 1989.

Mauries, Patrick. *Fornasetti: Designer of Dreams.* Boston: Bulfinch Press, 1991.

McDermott, Catherine. *Essential Design.* North Pomfret: Trafalgar Square, 1994.

McDonald, D. *Perspective Primer for Architects & Designers.* New York: Van Nostrand Reinhold, 1993.

Meehan, Aiden. *Celtic Design: The Tree of Life.* New York: Thames & Hudson, 1995.

Metropolis (Bellerophon, New York).

Mitchell, C. Thomas. *Redefining Designing: From Form to Experience.* New York: Van Nostrand Reinhold, 1993.

Morita, Akio, et al. *Made in Japan: Akio Morita & SONY.* New York: NAL/Dutton, 1989.

Mowl, Timothy. *Elizabethan & Jacobean Style.* San Francisco: Chronicle Books, 1993.

Norman, Donald A. *Design of Everyday Things.* New York: Doubleday & Co., Inc., 1990.

Nuehart, John. *Eames Design: The Work of the Office of Charles and Ray Eames.* New York: Harry N. Abrams, 1989.

O'Gorman, James F. *Three American Architects: Richardson, Sullivan and Wright, 1865–1915.* Chicago: University of Chicago Press, 1992.

Pearce, Chris. *Twentieth Century Design Classics.* London: Bloomsbury, 1987.

Pevsner, Nikolaus. *Pioneers of Modern Design from William Morris to Walter Gropius.* New York: Museum of Modern Art, 1949.

Pile, John. *Dictionary of Twentieth Century Design.* New York: Da Capo Press, 1994.

Quon, Michael. *Non-Traditional Design.* Glen Cove: PBC International, Inc., 1993.

Ricci, Stefania, & Edward Maedor. *Salvatore Ferragamo: Art of the Shoe 1896–1960.* New York: Rizzoli International Publications, Inc., 1992.

Ricman, Timothy D., & Jean M. Burks. *The Complete Book of Shaker Furniture.* New York: Harry N. Abrams, Inc., 1993.

Roberts, Jennifer D. *Norman Bel Geddes: An Exhibition of Theatrical & Industrial Designs.* Austin: University of Texas, Harry Ransom Humanities Research Center, 1979.

Rose, Cynthia. *Design after Dark.* New York: Thames & Hudson, 1993.

Schweiger, Werner J. *Wiener Werkstätte: Design in Vienna, 1903–1932.* New York: Abbeville Press, Inc., 1990.

Slafer, Anna, & Kevin Cahill. *Why Design? Projects from the National Building Museum.* Chicago: Chicago Review Press, Inc., 1995.

Smith, Terry. *Making the Modern: Industry, Art & Design in America.* Chicago: University of Chicago Press, 1994.

Sparke, Penny. *Design in Context.* London: Bloomsbury, 1987.

Bibliography ... Index

—. *Design in Italy: Eighteen-Seventy to the Present.* New York: Abbeville Press, Inc., 1988.

—. *The New Design Source Book.* London: Little Brown, 1992.

Sparke, Penny, ed. *The Plastics Age: From Bakelite to Beanbags & Beyond.* New York: Overlook Press, 1994.

Stansky, Peter. *Redesigning the World: William Morris, The 1880's and the Arts & Crafts.* Princeton: Princeton University Press, 1984.

Starck, Philippe. *Philippe Starck.* Cologne: Benedikt Taschen, 1991.

Stickley, Gustav. *Craftsman Homes: Architecture and Furnishings of the American Arts & Crafts Movement.* Reprinted. New York: Dover Publications, Inc., 1979.

Venturi, Robert. *Complexities and Contradictions in Modern Architecture.* 1966.

Venturi, Robert, Denise Scott Brown, & Steven Izenour. *Learning from Las Vegas.* Cambridge: MIT Press, 1972.

Walker, John A. *Glossary of Art, Architecture & Design since 1945.* New York: G. K. Hall & Co.

Walsh, Vivien. *Winning by Design: Technology, Product Design & International Competitiveness.* Cambridge: Blackwell Publishers, 1992.

Wolfe, Tom. *From Bauhaus to Our House.* New York: Washington Square Press, 1986.

Subject index

Abstraction-Creation 71
Academy for Design, Ulm 120, 128
academy of art 21
administrative reforms 22
advertising 14, 109
aesthetic 13
affluent society 129
alternative design 143
American way of life 98, 105, 108f., 110
antidesign 136, 140
applied arts 10
art 18, 26
Art Deco 88–95
art guild 42
art nouveau 30, 43–48, 51–54, 57, 89
art school 21
artist colony 39
Arts and Crafts Exhibition Society 43
arts and crafts movement 30, 41, 42, 49, 60, 74
assembly 12
automobile industry 31
avant-garde 64–85

Bakelite 93, 103, 137
Barcelona 53
Baroque 33
Bauhaus 57, 65, 68, 74–80, 122
Belle Epoque 47
bentwood chairs 34, 36
bentwood furniture 36f.
Biedermeier 22, 25ff., 116
bioform 102
Blood and Soil ideology 99
breech pistol (revolver) 30
building block system 78, 131
built-in kitchen 80

CAD/CAM 169
CIAM (Congrès International de l'Architecture Moderne) 71
Coca-Cola 105, 111
color theory 13
communication 15, 17
Compasso d'Oro 114, 115, 133, 135
conceptual art 18
Congress of Vienna 20, 22, 25
constructivism 64–67, 70, 89, 122
consultant designer 135
consumer society 140
consumption behavior 129
corporate culture 63, 173
corporate identity 9, 63, 135, 170, 173
corporate image 129
counterculture 141, 158
Cranbrook Academy of Art 93, 106, 107
crisis of functionalism 141f.
Crystal Palace 34, 35, 45
cubism 89

Dadaists 68
De Stijl 65, 68, 70ff., 75, 82, 122
decorative style 43
Design History Society 7
design management 14, 19
Design Workshop Berlin 161
development of taste 12
disegno 10
division of labor 29
domestic culture 27
Dresden Workshop 60
dwelling reform movement 40

Ecole Nationale des Arts Décoratifs 46
ecologal design 174
ecology 156
Eiffel Tower 28, 34, 35, 45
Empire style 26

Index

enlightenment 122
environment 174
environmental pollution 41
environmental tolerability 19
ergonomics 14, 17, 131, 170
escalator 34
Exposition Internationale des Arts Décoratifs, Paris 88
Expressionism 74

fashion 26
fashion design 16
finished pieces 21
firms
  Adler 130
  AEG 53, 62–63, 173
  Alessi 114, 134, 151, 152, 154
  Alfa Romeo 113
  Arabia 125
  Arflex 114
  Artek 85
  Artemide 134, 135, 136, 161
  AT&T 149
  Axor 175
  B&B Italia 135
  Bandalasta 93
  Bayer Leverkusen 141
  Bieffeplast 139
  Bloomingdale's 106, 107
  BMW 121
  Boeing 09
  Bofinger 122
  Bonwit Teller 107
  BP (British Petroleum) 111
  Braun 121, 122, 123, 129, 130, 132-133, 134
  Brionvega 114, 134, 135
  Cadillac 108
  Cappellini 114, 161
  Cassina 54, 70, 72, 84, 114, 115, 135, 154
  Classicon 91
  Coca-Cola 154
  Compagnie Générale du Métropolitain 46

Daum 47
Driade 162
Duravit 175
Electrolux 118
Erco 121, 167
Exxon 111
Ferrari 113
Fiat 113, 115, 134, 135
Flos 114
Ford 64, 98
Fritz Hansen 125, 127
frogdesign 16, 170
FSB 161
General Electric Company 62, 108
General Motors 98
Gestetner 110, 111
Gmund, Paper Factory 174
Habit 25
Hoesch 175
Hoover 109
Iitala 125, 126
Jena Glass Works 130
Junghans 120
Kartell 114, 115, 137–139
Kodak 98, 123
Knoll International 82, 107
Krupp 40
Krups 133
Lamy 135
Lancia 113
La Rinascente 115, 134
Lufthansa 17, 123
Macy's 110
Mauser 120
Mercedes Benz 134, 170
Miller, Herman 106, 107, 109, 137
Mitsubishi 154
Molteni 114
Morris & Co. 41, 42
Northwoods Company 93
Olivetti 113, 134, 135, 136, 154
Omega 120

Opel 50, 101, 102
de Padova 25
Pavoni 113
Pelikan Corporation 67
Pfitzenmaier, R. 117
Piaggio 112
Pininfarina 113
Pirelli 134
Poltrona Frau 114
Rasch 76, 152
Remington 30
Ritzenhoff 161
Rosenthal 122, 130
Rowenta 133
Shell 110, 111
Siemens 62
Singer 30
Sony 148, 168f.
Swatch 152, 171
Tecno 114, 115
Telefunken 133
Texaco 98
Thomas 130
Thonet 34, 36f., 57, 76
Vitra 107, 152, 156, 161, 172, 173
Vitsoe 130
Westinghouse 62, 109, 110
WMF 50, 130
Zanotta 114, 115
Forum Design 153, 156
free-swinging chair 83, 85
functionalism 13, 17, 18, 23, 74, 82, 100, 127, 128, 140, 141, 158, 163
functions of design 16, 17
furniture for workers 40

garden city 38, 40, 54
Gelsenkirch Baroque 116
geometry 13
German Work Alliance/Union (Werkbund) 30, 38, 46, 51, 54, 56, 57, 60f., 100, 117
Glasgow School of Art 54f.
good form 119f., 130, 131, 134, 148, 158, 162

Index

graphic design 13, 15, 16
Great Depression 64, 86, 97
Greyhound 111
guild regulations 23

Health Exhibition, 1930 Dresden 67
health reform movement 40
historicism 34, 39
history of design 19, 40, 156, 172
Hollywood 86, 95, 112
homeland protection movement 40

Indore, Palace 91f.
industrial design 13, 14
industrial revolution 10, 12
industrialization 10, 12, 20, 21, 26, 38, 41, 54, 64, 112
International Building Exhibition, 1927 Stuttgart 72
international style 83–85, 104–105
iron production 28
Italy. The New Domestic Landscape 136

kidney table 118
kitsch 149, 151,159

La Sagrada Familia 52, 53
Lambretta 113
land reform movement 40
literature 26
Lomonossov Porcelain Factory 68, 70
Lucky Strike 105, 110, 111

machine furniture 49
mainstream design 134
marketing 14, 109
Marshall Plan 104
mass production (industrial) 29, 39, 41, 52, 60, 92, 100
Mathildenhöhe 50
mechanization 30

melamine 118, 119, 154
microelectronics 151, 156, 168
Middle Ages 75
Minimal Art 128, 146
Möbel perdu 158, 159
modern 57, 127
modernism 13
Modernismo 53
Moskwitch 111
Munich Workshops 50, 62
Museum of Modern Art, New York 83, 85, 136

nature protection movement 40
neo-Baroque 159, 165
neo-functionalism 130
New Age 148
New Bauhaus 77, 79
New Design 138, 156, 157–166
nylon 137

oil crisis 139, 140, 145
Organic Design in Home Furnishings 106
ornament 13, 44, 45, 46, 52
ornamentation 44, 47

patent 14
patented furniture 31
pattern books 20, 21
Pennsylvania Railroad Company 96, 111
People's Radio 103
Pestalozzi 122
phenol resin 93
photography 16
plant designs 44
polyester 137
polypropylene 137
polystyrol 137
polyurethane 137
pop art 130, 141, 144, 146
pop music 130, 144
postmodern, Postmodern movement 17, 89, 141, 148, 149

Pre-Raphaelites 40, 42
Presse, 1928 Cologne 67
proportion 13f.
Protest movements 129
prototype 18, 159
pseudo-classicism 99
psychology 17
Pullmann car 30
punk 155, 156
puritanism 71

Radical Design 146
ready-made 27, 114, 159, 160
reconstruction 104
recycling design 144
redesign 153
reform of commercial art 41
reform movement 12, 29, 34, 39, 54
Renaissance 33

sales catalogs 21
satellite community 131
Scholl Family Foundation 120
School of Nancy 47
Schröder House, Utrecht 73
Secessionist Exhibit, Eighth 55, 56
semiotics 13, 17
service design 19, 171
Shaker 20, 23–25
Skandinavia 125f.
socialism 39, 41, 69
standardization 13, 66
steam engine 20, 37, 47
steel-framed skyscrapers 92
Stile Liberty 43
streamlined form 97–98, 102, 119
Studebaker 111
student movements 130
styling 17, 97, 142, 169
suprematism 65, 68, 69

teak 126
technical physics 13
Terence Conran Foundation 172

Index

total work of art (Gesamt-kunstwerk) 45, 46

utopia 140, 144

veneer 26
Vespa 112, 113
Victorian Era 34
Vienna Workshops
   (Werkstätte) 30, 57
Visiona, 1969 Cologne 145
Vitra Design Museum 173
Volkskultur (folk culture) 99
Volkswagen 101–102

Walkman 168
WCHUTEIN 68
WCHUTEMAS 68
Weimar 51
Weissenhof Settlement,
   Stuttgart 79, 81
Werkbund debate 60, 61
Werkbund Exhibition 60,
   61, 81, 117
Wirtschaftswunder 116, 117
worker settlements 40
workers' barracks 28, 40
workers' union movement
   38, 39
world exhibition 34, 38
   Barcelona 82, 86
   Brussels 128
   Chicago 34
   London 20, 31, 35
   Munich 34
   New York 96, 98
   Paris 28, 34, 35, 86, 99
   Philadelphia 25, 28, 30
   St. Louis 34
   Vienna 34

Index of names

Aalto, Alvar 85, 126, 142
Adamovich, Mikhail 68
Adorno, Theodor 141, 142
Aicher, Otl 121, 123
Albers, Josef 78–79
Albus, Volker 159
Alchimia 140, 147, 151–
   154
Aldrin, Edwin 128, 129
Andersen, Aagaard 137
Ando, Tadao 173
Arad, Ron 160, 161, 162
Archizoom Associati 147
Arens, Gerd 158
Argan, Giulio Carlo 136
Armstrong, Neil 128, 129
Arnold, Karl 60
Arp, Hans 71, 107
Arpke, Otto 86
Arribas, Alfredo 162
Astaire, Fred 86

Baekeland, Leo 93
Baker, Josephine 86, 87
Ball, Hugo 71
Bangert, Albrecht 156
Bartels, Heiko 158
Barthes, Roland 150
Bätzner, Helmut 138
Baudrillard, Jean 149
Beardsley, Aubrey V. 45
Bedin, Martine 154
Beethoven, Ludwig van 20
Behrens, Peter 39, 43, 49,
   50, 54, 60, 62-63, 75,
   79, 83, 173
Bel Geddes, Norman 96,
   98, 108
Bell, Alexander Graham 28,
   30
Bellini, Mario 135, 136, 173
Berlage, Hendrik Petrus 72
Bertoia, Harry 106, 107
Beuys, Joseph 9
Bialetti, Alfonso Renato 92

Bill, Max 120, 121, 122,
   123, 148
Bismarck, Otto von 28
Bofill, Ricardo 150
Böhm, Gottfried 150
Bonetti, Mattia 163, 164
Borngräber, Christian 159
Borsani, Osvaldo 115
Boulton, Matthew 28
Brandolini, Andreas 159
Brandt, Edgar 88, 90
Brandt, Marianne 76
Brandt, Willy 128
Branzi, Andrea 147, 151,
   153, 154
Breker, Arno 99
Breuer, Marcel 14, 75, 76,
   77, 78, 83, 84
Brevern, Renate von 158
Bugatti, Carlo 53
Burkhardt, François 15
Burne-Jones, Edward 42
Bush, George 148

Calder, Alexander 107
Capra, Fritjof 148
Cardin, Pierre 164
Carter, Jimmy 140
Cassandre (A. Mouron)
   87
Castelli, Giulio 138
Castelli-Ferrieri, Anna 138,
   139
Castiglioni, Achille 114
Castiglioni, Livio 114
Castiglioni, Pier Giacomo
   114
Cézanne, Paul 54
Chanel, Coco 86, 88, 91
Chareau, Pierre 90, 91
Charpentier, Alexandre 47,
   48
Chechonin, S. 68
Chia, Sandro 153
Chippendale, Thomas 22
Churchill, Winston 86
Citterio, Antonio 173
Clemente, Francesco 153
Clinton, Bill 148
Clotet, L. 162

Index

Cocktail 158, 159
Colani, Luigi 146
Cole, Henry 41
Colombo, Joe 138, 139, 145
Colt, Samuel 30
Courbet, Gustave 38
Crane, Walter 42, 43
Curie, Marie 28

Dalisi, Riccardo 151
D'Ascanio, Corradino 112
Daum, A. 47
da Vinci, Leonardo 11
Dean, James 104
Deganello, Paolo 147, 156
Delamare, Jacques 95
Dell, Christian 102
de Lucchi, Michele 139, 151, 153, 154
de Pas, Gionatan 144
Derrida, Jacques 149
Des-in 143, 144
Deskey, Donald 95
Diesel, Rudolf 28
Dixon, Tom 160, 161, 162
Doesburg, Theo van 65, 70, 71, 72, 73, 75
Dorfles, Gillo 136
Dorner, Marie-Christine 163, 164, 166
Dreyfuss, Henry 98, 108
Drocco, Guido 145
Dryden, Ernst Deutsch 86
Dubreuil, André 163
du Pasquier, Natalie 154
D'Urbino, Donato 144

Eames, Charles 8, 106, 107, 127, 173
Eames, Ray 8, 106
Eco, Umberto 136, 148, 149
Edison, Thomas Alva 30, 31
Eesteren, Cornelis van 65, 71, 74
Eichler, Fritz 132
Eiffel, Alexandre Gustave 35
Einstein, Albert 64

Endell, August 48, 49
Engels, Friedrich 20, 24
Ernst Ludwig, Grand Duke of Hesse 50
Ernst, Joseph Caspar 117

Factor Design 174
Feininger, Lyonel 74, 75
Feith, Michel 158
Feltus, Harlan Ross 16
Fiedler, Leslie 149
Filbinger, Hans 123, 124
Fischer, Hardy 158
Flaxman, John 21
Fleetwood, Roy 167
Ford, Henry 64
Foster, Norman 166, 167
Franklin, Benjamin 20
Freud, Sigmund 64

Gabo, Naum 66
Gagnère, Olivier 163
Gallé, Emile 46, 47
Garouste, Elizabeth 163, 164
Gatti, Piero 146
Gaudí, Antoni 52, 53, 114, 162
Gaultier, Jean-Paul 163, 164
Gavoille, Kristian 163
Gehry, Frank O. 173
Gershwin, George 86
Giedion, Siegfried 31
GINBANDE 158, 159, 160
Giugiaro, Giorgio 15
Global Tools 147, 152, 154
Goethe, Johann Wolfgang von 22
Grass, Günter 116
Graves, Michael 150, 151, 154
Gray, Eileen 90, 91
Gregotti, Vittorio 136
Gropius, Walter 54, 60, 61, 74, 75, 76, 77, 78, 79, 81, 121
Gros, Jochen 144
Gruppo 9999 147
Gsöllpointner, Helmuth 156

Guerriero, Alessandro 151, 152
Gugelot, Hans 120, 121, 122, 123, 132, 133
Guimard, Hector 46, 47, 48

Habermas, Jürgen 149
Hadid, Zaha M. 173
Hamilton, Richard 108
Hareiter, Angela 156
Haring, Keith 171
Haug, Wolfgang Fritz 142
Haussmann, Robert 151
Haussmann, Trix 151
Heartfield, John 103
Heine, Klaus-Achim 158
Heine, Thomas Theodor 48
Henningsen, Poul 127
Hepburn, Audrey 112
Hildinger, Paul 120
Hirche, Herbert 132, 133
Hitchcock, Henry-Russell 83, 84
Hitler, Adolf 64, 93, 99, 100, 102, 106
Hodler, Ferdinand 57
Hoff, Robert van't 71
Hoffmann, Josef 56, 57
Hollein, Hans 150, 154
Hood, Raymond 94
Horst, Katja 174
Horta, Victor 45, 46
Howard, Ebenezer 40
Hullmann, Harald 158
Hundertpfund, Jörg 160
Huszár, Vilmos 71
Huxley, Aldous 86

Isozaki, Arata 154
Itten, Johannes 75

Jacobsen, Arne 125, 127, 137
Jahn, Helmut 150
Jeanneret, Pierre 84
Jencks, Charles 148, 149, 150
Johnson, Philip 83, 84, 149, 150

Index

Jones, Owen 41
Jucker, Karl J. 76

Kahny, Albert 98
Kandinsky, Wassily 65, 66, 68, 78
Kersting, Georg Friedrich 26
Kersting, Walter Maria 103
Kessler, Harry Graf 51
King, Perry A. 135
Kjaerholm, Poul 125
Klee, Paul 75
Klimt, Gustav 55, 57
Klint, Kaare 125, 126
Klotz, Heinrich 149
Kok, Wim 71
Kramer, Ferdinand 80
Krier, Rob 150
Krohn, Lisa 168
Kunstflug 18, 158, 159, 169
Kuramata, Shiro 154, 157

Lalique, René 89, 90
Lang, Fritz 64
Lanvin, Jeanne 88, 91
La Pietra, Ugo 151
Laubersheimer, Wolfgang 158
Lawrie, Lee 94
Lebedew, Vladimir 68
Leck, Bart Anthony van der 71
Le Corbusier (Charles Edouard Jeanneret-Gris) 36, 81, 84, 89, 90, 91
Lecoute, Thierry 163
Lee, Ann 24
Leistler, Carl 36
Lenin, Vladimir Ilyich 64
Lichtenstein, Roy 141, 144
Lindbergh, Charles 86
Lindinger, Herbert 121, 123
Lissitzky, El 65-67, 71
Loewy, Raymond 96, 97, 98, 108, 110-111, 164
Lomazzi, Paolo 144
Loos, Adolf 13, 54, 56, 57, 83
Lyotard, Jean-François 149

Macdonald, Frances 56
Macdonald, Margaret 56
Mackintosh, Charles Rennie 54, 55, 56, 153
Mackmurdo, Arthur 43
MacNair, J. Herbert 56
Madonna 164
Majorelle, Louis 47, 48
Maldonado, Tomás 121, 123
Malevich, Kasimir 65, 67, 68
Mao Tse-tung 104
Marcks, Gerhard 75
Mare, André 89, 91
Mariscal, Javier 154, 162, 163
Marx, Karl 20, 28, 29
Mathsson, Bruno 124
Maurer, Ingo 143
McLuhan, Marshal 128
Meacham, Joseph 24
Mello, Franco 145
Memphis 139, 151, 153-156, 160, 161, 162, 163
Mendini, Alessandro 151, 152, 154, 171
Metternich, Clemens Wenzel von 36
Meyer, Adolf 61
Meyer, Hannes 77-79
Meyer-Voggenreiter, Detlef 158
Mies van der Rohe, Ludwig 60, 79, 81, 82, 83, 84
Milá, Alfonso 162
Millet, Jean-François 38
Mitscherlich, Alexander 142
Moholy-Nagy, László 75f., 77, 79, 130
Mollino, Carlo 114, 115
Mondrian, Piet 70, 71, 72
Monet, Claude 28
Moore, Charles 150
Moore, Henry 106, 107, 108
Morgue, Oliver 141
Morita, Akio 168
Morris, William 38, 40, 41, 42, 43, 45, 64, 173

Morrison, Jasper 160, 161, 162, 173
Morse, Samuel 20
Moser, Koloman 55, 56, 57
Muche, Georg 75
Mühlhaus, Heike 158
Mukarovsky, Jan 16
Müller, Reinhard 158
Mussolini, Benito 86
Muthesius, Eckart 91, 92
Muthesius, Hermann 13, 56, 60

Napoleon Bonaparte 20
Nasarevskaya, Marya 69
Natta, Giulio 137
Naumann, Friedrich 60
Nehls, Wolfgang 142
Nelson, George 154, 173
Nemo 163
Nietzsche, Friedrich 54
Nizzoli, Marcello 113, 152
Nobel, Alfred 28
Noguchi, Isamu 109

Obrist, Hermann 48, 49
Ohl, Herbert 123
Olbrich, Joseph Maria 39, 50
Oliva, Achille Bonito 149
One Off Ltd. 160-161, 162
Ortner, Laurids 156
Osthaus, Karl Ernst 46, 51, 60
Oud, Jacobus Johannes Pieter 71, 72, 81, 91

Paladino, Mimmo 153, 171
Pankok, Bernhard 49
Panton, Verner 125, 127, 128, 137
Paolini, Cesare 146
Patout, Pierre 88
Paul, Bruno 49
Paxton, Joseph 35
Peck, Gregory 112
Pentagon 158
Perriand, Charlotte 84
Pesce, Gaetano 156
Pevsner, Anton 66

Index

Piano, Renzo 166
Picasso, Pablo 54, 86, 162
Piretti, Giancarlo 134, 135
Ponti, Gió 113, 115, 134
Popova, Ljubov 68
Porsche, Ferdinand 101
Prouvé, Jean 90, 91
Prouvé, Victor 47
Pullman, G. M. 30
Putman, Andrée 163

Quant, Mary 144

Radice, Barbara 154
Raizer, L. J. 69
Rams, Dieter 129, 132, 133
Raphael 40
Rateau, Armand-Albert 90
Rathenau, Emil 62
Redon, Odilon 45
Remington, P. 30
Richter, Adrian Ludwig 25
Riemerschmid, Richard 49, 61
Rietveld, Gerrit Thomas 70, 71, 72, 73, 75, 152
Rodchenko, Alexander 65, 66, 67, 69
Rodin, Auguste 45
Roericht, Hans 122, 123
Rogers, Richard 166
Rogoshin, N. 66
Rohbeck, Sylvia 160
Röhl, Karl-Peter 74
Rosanova, Olga 68
Roschdestvenski, Constantin 68
Rossetti, Dante Gabriel 38, 40
Rossi, Aldo 150
Roth, Alfred 83
Roth, Emil 83
Ruhlmann, Jacques-Emile 88, 89, 90
Ruskin, John 42

Saarinen, Eero 93, 106, 107
Sapper, Richard 134, 136, 138

Schiaparelli, Elsa 91
Schiller, Friedrich 20
Schinkel, Karl Friedrich 21
Schlemmer, Oskar 75
Schmidt, Karl 60
Schneider-Esleben, Claudia 158, 159
Schreiner, Frank 159
Schütte-Lihotzky, Margarete 80
Schwitters, Kurt 71
Scolari, Carla 144
Seeger, Mia 118
Semper, Gottfried 35, 41
Severini, Gino 71
Sheraton, Thomas 20, 22
Shire, Peter 155
Shreve, Lamb & Harman 94
Singer, Isaac 30
Sipek, Borek 157
SITE 149
Slezin, S. 167
Sloterdijk, Peter 149
Sontag, Susan 140
Sotnikov, Alexei Georgiewitsch 66
Sottsass, Ettore 8, 135, 147, 151, 153, 154, 155, 157
Speer, Albert 99
Spitzweg, Carl 25
Stalin, Joseph 69
Stam, Mart 77
Starck, Philippe 8, 139, 163, 164, 165, 166, 173, 175
Stepanova, Varvarya 68
Stiletto (Frank Schreiner) 159, 160
Stirling, James 150
Strum 146, 147
Studio Per 162
Süe, Louis 89, 91
Sujetin, Nikolai Mikhailovich 68
Sullivan, Louis Henry 8, 23, 58, 59
Superstudio 147
Syniuga, Siegfried Michael 9, 159, 160

Tatlin, Vladimir 64–66
Teague, Walter Dorwin 96, 98, 108
Teodoro, Franco 146
Thimonnier, Barthélemy 30
Thonet brothers 12, 37
Thonet, Michael 36
Thun, Matteo 8, 139, 154, 155, 167, 171
Tiffany, Louis Comfort 47
Totem 163
Tusquets Blanca, Oscar 162, 163

Valin, Eugène 47
Van Alen, William 94
Vantongerloo, Georges van 71
Velde, Henry Clément van de 44, 45, 46, 50, 51, 60, 74
Venturi, Robert 149, 150
Victoria, Queen 28

Wagenfeld, Wilhelm 76, 130, 132
Wagner, Otto 50, 55, 56, 57
Wagner, Richard 38
Warhol, Andy 140, 144
Watt, James 20, 28
Webb, Philip 42
Wedgwood, Josiah 21
Wegner, Hans J. 125, 126
Welsch, Wolfgang 149
Wesselmann, Tom 144
Wilhelm Ernst, Grand Duke of Weimar 51
Wils, Jan 71
Wright brothers 54
Wright, Frank Lloyd 8, 54, 58, 59, 65, 71, 72, 83, 92, 107
Würndorfer, Fritz 57

Zanuso, Marco 134, 135, 138
Zevi, Bruno 118
Ziegler, Henry 106, 107
Ziegler, Karl Waldemar 137

Picture credits

AEG, Frankfurt 62-3
Alchimia Studio, Milano 152t+b, 153t
Alessi (tea kettle with whistle in the shape of a bird made of 18/10 stainfree steel by Alessi s.p.a., Crusinallo, Italy. Design Michael Graves 1985) 151b
Angelo Hornak Library, London 42c, 94bl, 95
Aram Designs Ltd., London 91t+c
Architectural Ass., London 94br
Archiv f. Kunst und Geschichte, Berlin 42b, 47br, 87br, 104, 105b, 129c
Artek Oy, Helsinki 65b
Artemide Deutschland, Düsseldorf 136c
Asenbaum, Paul, Wien 57
Ballo, Aldo, Mailand 146b
Bangert Vlg., München 109b, 120t
Bauhausarchiv, Berlin 14, 74, 75t+b, 76, 77tl, 78, 79, 81b
Bayer AG, Leverkusen 128b, 145t
Biblioteca Ambrosiana, Milano 11
Bibliothek der Landesgewerbeanstalt Bayern, Nürnberg 40
Bildarchiv Foto Marburg 44r, 45t, 50, 80t, 81t
Bonham's Knightsbridge, London 139b
Braun AG, Kronberg 129t, 132-3
Bridgeman Art Library, London 58b, 59b
Brionvega s.p.a., Milano 134
Büttenpapierfabrik, Gmund 174b
Capellini, Milano 160ct, 161bl
Carl Ernst Osthaus-Museum, Hagen 51b
Cassina, Meda 54, 55b, 56t, 59t, 70b, 84t+b, 115c
Castelli, Ahlen 135c
Christie's, New York 89t+b
ClassiCon, München 91b
Design Council, London 93b, 113t
Design Museum, London 118b, 172
Deutsche Bahn, Köln 169b
Deutscher Werkbund, Frankfurt 61c, 117t
Deutsches Museum, München 28, 29b, 32t
Dorner, Marie-Christine, Paris 166t
DPA, Köln 128b
Driade, Milano 162b
Driade–Stefan Müller GmbH, München 157b
Duravit, Hornberg 175
Ellenberg, Peter W., Freiburg 36b (photo: Kai Mewes, München), 37b
Erco Leuchten, Lüdenscheid 167t
Eta Lazi Studios, Stuttgart 117
Feldman, Ronald, New York 149t
Finster, Hans, Zürich 83b
Foster, Norman, London 166b
Foto Ulrich, Völklingen 100b
frogdesign, Altensteig 16b, 170b
Fruitlands Museum, Harvard 230

Galerie B. Bischofberger, Zürich 114b
Gamma, Vanves 164t
Gastinger, Mario, München 48t
Gebr. Thonet GmbH, Frankenberg 12b, 77b, 83t
General Motors, Detroit 98b
Gil Amiaga 149b
Gnamm, Sophie-Renate, Buch am Erlbach 46, 47bl, 61b
Grundmann, Jürgen, München 82c
Gufram/Fr. Timpanaro, Köln 145c
Guggenheim Museum, New York 107c
H. Armstrong Roberts Inc., Philadelphia 108c, 109t
Hancock Shaker Village, Pittsfield 23b, 24t
Haus der Geschichte der Bundes-republik Deutschland, Bonn 119b
HfG, Offenbach 143b
International Licensing Partners, Amsterdam (©1994 ABC/Mondrian Estate/Holtzman Trust. licensed by ILP) 70t
Kartell, Noviglio 138
Klein, Dan, London 89c, 90t, 94t
Knoll International, Murr 82, 106
Kolodziej, Idris, Berlin 159, 160, 161
Krohn, Lisa, New York 168
Kunstflug, Düsseldorf 18, 169
Kunsthalle Tübingen 108
Kunstmuseum Düsseldorf 139
Küthe, Erich, Remscheid 2, 19
Lesieutre, Alain, Paris 53b
Loewy, Viola, L'Annonciade, Monte Carlo 96, 97, 111
Lufthansa, Köln 17, 86
M. A. S., Barcelona 52
Mariscal, Javier, Barcelona 163
Maurer, Ingo, München 143
Memphis, Milano 151t, 153b, 154b, 155t+b
Mercedes Benz AG, Stuttgart 170
Moholy, Lucia 77r
Moore, Charles W., Los Angeles 150
Morrison, Jasper, London 161
Münchner Stadtmuseum 25b, 48b
Musée de la Publicité, Paris 87tr
Musée des Arts Décoratifs (Nissim de Camondo), Paris 47t, 87bl, 88b
Museum für Kunsthandwerk, Frankfurt 51t
Museum of Modern Art, New York 49tl, 67b (Alfred H. Barr Jr. Papers), Tecno, Milano 167b
Nationalmuseum, Warschau 26
Niederecker, Ursula, Galerie am Herzogplatz, München 22t
Nordenfeldske Kunstindustrimuseum, Trondheim 45b
Olivetti Synthesis, Milano 113c (Marcello Nizzoli, 1950), 135br (Werbung Ettore Sottsass & Roberto

Pieraccini, 1969) + l (Ettore Sott-sass, 1969), 136t (Mario Bellini, 1973)
Österr. Nationalbibliothek, Wien 56
Oudsten, Frank den, Amsterdam 71c+b, 72t+b, 73c+b
Pelikan Kunstarchiv, Hannover 67t
Petersen, Knut Peter, Berlin 110b
Piaggio, Mailand 112t
Poltronova, Montale 150b
Reisenthel, Katja Horst, Puchheim 174
Rijksdienst Beeldende Kunst, Amsterdam 65br, 73t
Ron Arad Associates, London 160t (Foto: Christoph Kicherer)
Ross Feltus, Harlan, Düsseldorf 16t
Sammlung Jäger, Düsseldorf 119t
Selle, Gert 103t
Shell International Petroleum Company Ltd., London 110t
SIDI, Barcelona (© B. D. Ediciones de Diseñó) 162c
Singer 30t
Sonnabend Gallery, New York 90b
Sony Europa, Köln 168b
Sotheby's, London 92t
Sottsass, Ettore, Milano 147b, 154t, 155c
Stadt Gelsenkirchen 116
Stadtmuseum Köln 100
Stahlmach, Adelbert, Berlin 25t, 27
Starck, Philippe 8, 164c+b, 165t+b
Stiftung Weimarer Klassik 22b
Strobel, Peter, Köln 158l
Suomen Rakennustaiteen Museo, Helsinki 85t
Swatch, Biel 171
Syniuga, Siegfried Michael 9
Photoarchiv C. Raman Schlemmer, Oggebbio 75tl
Tecta, Lauenförde 90c
The Henry Moore Foundation, Hertfordshire 107b
Transglobe Agency, Hamburg 144t
Ullstein Bilderdienst, Berlin 34
University of Texas, Austin 96tl+tr
Verlag Gerd Hatje, Ostfildern/Mang, Karl, Wien 141b, 148
VG Bild-Kunst, Bonn 39t, 65t, 67c, 72c, 84c, 87tr, 108b, 158/9b
Victoria&Albert Museum, London 35t
Vitra, Weil am Rhein 106b, 107t, 135t, 137, 152bl, 156t+b, 157t, 160bc+b, 173
Voiello 15
Volkswagen, Wolfsburg 101, 102b
WMF, Geislingen 130t
Zanotta, Nuova Milanese 144b (Mauro Masera), 146t (Marino Ramazzotti), 114t+c, 115t (all three photos Masera, Milan)